WBN

# Texas Women
# Who Dared
# to be
# First

# TEXAS WOMEN
## Who Dared to be First

## JEAN FLYNN

EAKIN PRESS ⟨EP⟩ Austin, Texas

FIRST EDITION

Copyright © 1999
By Jean Flynn

Published in the United States of America
By Eakin Press
An Imprint of Sunbelt Media, Inc.
P.O. Drawer 90159  ★   Austin, TX 78709-0159
email eakinpub@sig.net
www.eakinpress.com

2  3  4  5  6  7  8  9  10

ISBN 1-57168-232-5

**Library of Congress Cataloging-in-Publication Data**

Flynn, Jean.
    Women Firsts:  Texas women who dared to be different /
by Jean Flynn.
        p.   cm.
    Includes bibliographical references and index.
    Summary:  Profiles notable women in Texas who challenged the struc-
ture of society to succeed in a male-dominated world, including
Christina V. Daniels Adair, Mary Austin Holley, and Judith Zaffirini.
        ISBN 1-57168-232-5
        1. Women—Texas—Biography-Juvenile literature.
    2. Women—Texas—History—juvenile literature.
    [ 1. Women—Texas—Biography.  2. Texas—Biography.  3. Sex role.]
    I. Title
HQ1438. T4F59  1998
305.4'092'2764—dc21                                           98-29870
                                                                   CIP
                                                                   AC

# For The Renegade Club

Katherine Baxter
Robin Black
Kay Cavanaugh
Millie DeAnda
Shirley Elrod
Diana Carroll-Wirth
Bonnie Flake
Wanda Herron
Barbara Higdon
Shirley Huffman
Nancy Klepper
Treysa McKinney
Ann McMullan
Mary Middleton
Olga Roper
Saralda Ross
Barbara Stanush
Nedra Voorhies
Elaine Wagener
Susan Walter
Kiddo Wright
and my daughter, Deirdre Siobhan Bass

# Contents

# Preface

The women included in this book are but a few who made inroads for all Texas women in male-dominated positions. Many of the women who succeeded were encouraged by their husbands and children. Some felt they could not marry and achieve a career at the same time, so they remained single. Two-career families are common in Texas today. Many women have proved that a mother can have a successful career and not neglect her family.

Texans are indebted to the strong, determined women who challenged society's structure and gave us role models to follow. They were the first but not the last, as young men and women continue to cross gender barriers to make Texas a place of job opportunities.

*Christia V. Daniels Adair*

# CHRISTIA V. DANIELS ADAIR
## October 22, 1893 - December 31, 1989

**A TEXAS FIRST AS CIVIL RIGHTS ACTIVIST AND SUFFRAGIST**

Christia Adair was one of the few black women active in the Texas suffrage movement and the most outspoken. Adair co-founded the Harris County Democrats, an integrated alternative to the county's segregated Democratic organization. She was one of the first two African-Americans elected to the state Democratic committee. Christia was also the first black woman to demand equal rights to women's dressing rooms in department stores.

### Early Standards

"My parents set a standard I had to stretch to reach," Adair said.

Hardy and Ada Daniels set high standards for all of their children. Born on October 22, 1893, in Victoria, Texas, Christia was one of four children. The Daniels lived in the small town of Edna, where their children attended a small elementary school for blacks only. The Daniels did not depend on the school alone to educate their children.

Every evening Mr. Daniels had the children sit around the table for a discussion of current political events. Young Christia thought it was very boring. She soon learned that taking part in the discussion was a family responsibility. Her father expected her to take an active role and to be knowledgeable about politics. That training was the beginning of Christia's interest in politics and her feelings of responsibility to be involved in political decisions.

*"We dressed up and went to vote, and when we got down there, well, we couldn't vote. [July 27, 1918] . . . that just hurt our hearts real bad . . . "*
— Christia Adair

**Church Leader**

Mrs. Daniels was very active in Scruggs Chapel Methodist Church. She wanted her children to help with whatever they were asked to do. Christia helped at church suppers and meetings. Soon she was accepting a leadership role in the church.

Miss Beulah, the superintendent of the Sunday school at their church, became ill with tuberculosis. She called for sixteen-year-old Christia to come to see her. "I want you to be superintendent of the Sunday school," she told Christia.

"Oh, Miss Beulah, I don't know how to be a superintendent!" Christia exclaimed.

"You can learn," Miss Beulah insisted. She kept insisting until Christia promised she would take the job. Christia became the youngest female in Texas to be superintendent of a Sunday school.

## Education

Mr. and Mrs. Daniels had never gone to school, but they wanted their children to get a good education. Christia went to the small elementary school in Edna until 1910. Just before her seventeenth birthday she went to Austin with her brother to finish high school at Sam Huston College (now Huston-Tillotson College), a normal school for blacks. After high school, she enrolled at an all-black state college, Prairie View State Normal and Industrial College (now known as Prairie View A&M). After graduation, she returned to Edna to teach at her old elementary school.

Teachers did not make much money, and of all the teachers, black women teachers made the least amount. Mr. Daniels talked Christia into moving to nearby Vanderbilt, where she could make a better salary. In Vanderbilt she made $40 a month, and she met her future husband, handsome Elbert Adair.

## Marriage

Elbert Adair and Christia Daniels were married in May 1918. Elbert was a brakeman for the Missouri Pacific Railroad. Soon the couple moved to Kingsville in South Texas. Kingsville's 7,000 residents lived in segregated neighborhoods for blacks, whites, and Hispanics. Elbert did not want his wife to work outside the home. There were few cultural or social activities for an educated young black woman, so Christia filled her time with volunteer work.

The first thing she did was to organize a Sunday school class for the children. The black church had no

Sunday school. Then one day when she saw one of the teenage boys from her Sunday school class coming out of a gambling house, she waged a war against the sheriff. The gambling house was located on the edge of the black community or, as it was called in 1918, Negro Town. The sheriff was being paid to ignore the house, even though gambling was illegal. The black citizens felt helpless to do anything about it until Adair saw her Sunday school student there.

"It just put war-fire in me . . . and I found that he wasn't the only teenager that they were using at the tables, to make money," Adair later said. She knew the black women could not change things alone. She went to the president of the Mothers Club in the white community. The woman suggested that the black women form a Mothers Club and that the two groups work together. It was the first interracial Mothers Club organized, and it got results.

When the sheriff heard that the mothers, black and white, were organized, he became frightened. He called a lot of women to his office and held court. No one would tell him anything. The mothers finally went to the district attorney to complain about the sheriff's treatment of them. In the end, the sheriff had to close the gambling house and nail boards over the windows and doors of the gambling house himself.

**Politics**

The campaign against the sheriff was so successful that Adair became a suffragist, one of the few black suffragists in the state. She worked with white groups to win

4

the right to vote. Not all women were for women voters, though. An anti-suffrage movement was organized in 1916. The Texas Association Opposed to Woman Suffrage was supported by former governor Oscar B. Colquitt.

Colquitt said in the 1916 senate race, "Some men say, 'My wife can cast as intelligent a vote as the Negro and Mexican.' That is not the question. Probably she can cast a more intelligent vote than her husband who says it, but the point is that when you give the ballot to women, you give it to all women, regardless of color."

Adair was aware of the opposition to women, especially black women, having the right to vote. But she did not know that the passage of the Nineteenth Amendment that gave women the right to vote in primary elections did not apply to black women. She was very hurt when she was turned away from the election polling place. But the experience made her more determined to fight for her rights.

An incident in Kingsville in 1920 influenced Adair to begin her lifetime work in racial reform. When Adair heard that presidential candidate Warren G. Harding was stopping in Kingsville, she took a small group of black children to see him. She arrived at the railway platform early and put her children next to where Harding was to speak. The children were very excited and could hardly wait to shake hands with such a prominent person. After his speech, Harding reached over the black children to shake hands with the white children behind them. He pretended the black children were not there.

"I was offended and insulted and I made up my mind I wouldn't be a Republican ever," she recalled.

## NAACP

In 1925 the Adairs moved to Houston, where Christia Adair joined a new branch of the National Association for the Advancement of Colored People (NAACP). The NAACP was organized to fight discrimination against blacks. The group challenged laws that were unfair and unconstitutional, and checked to see that existing laws protected blacks as well as whites.

After Elbert Adair died in 1943, Mrs. Adair spent all of her time working for the NAACP. She served as executive secretary for twelve years. During that time blacks won the right to vote in primary elections as well as general elections (1944). But Adair and the NAACP paid a price for that right. The 1940s and 1950s were frightening years for Adair. The NAACP offices received many bomb threats, and Adair received many death threats. Her friends begged her to resign for her own safety. When she would not resign, they begged her to buy a gun. "I never had a gun . . . but they thought I did. I did a lot of big talking," Adair later said.

In 1957 the Houston police tore up the NAACP office looking for a membership list. Adair said repeatedly that she did not have such a list. The Houston chapter of the NAACP disbanded and Adair resigned as executive secretary in 1959. She later helped rebuild the branch to 10,000 members. She also helped desegregate the Houston Public Library, as well as the airport, city buses, and the veterans' hospital. Blacks soon became eligible to serve on juries, and newspapers started referring to blacks with the same titles they used for whites. Also, blacks were hired for the first time by the county government.

## An Expensive Girdle

Adair desegregated women's dressing rooms when she insisted on using a room reserved for white women only. Blacks were not allowed to try on clothes in department stores. If they bought something that did not fit, they were stuck with it. The stores would not accept the return of a garment that had been tried on by a black person. Adair decided it was time black customers were treated with the same respect as white customers.

Although she was very thin, she went to a department store and selected an expensive girdle. She insisted on trying it on, and finally the manager allowed Adair in a dressing room. "I bought a $27.50 girdle which I *did not* need to establish the right of Negro women to try on garments," she said. She kept the girdle and achieved her purpose. Black customers began using dressing rooms.

## An Activist to the End

Adair co-founded the Harris County Democrats, an integrated Democratic organization. She was one of the first blacks in Houston to serve as a precinct judge. In 1966 she was one of the first two blacks elected to the state Democratic committee, and she was the first black woman elected to the board of the Methodist Episcopal Church. She worked as a county clerk of absentee voting until she was in her eighties.

Adair was one of fifty black women interviewed for an oral history of black women. A county park was dedicated to her on her eighty-fourth birthday. In 1984 she was inducted into the first Texas Women's Hall of Fame.

Christia V. Daniels Adair far outreached the standard her parents set for her. She not only expanded her life and the lives of those around her, but she also expanded the lives of black Texans for generations to come. An activist all of her ninety-five years, she died a quiet death on December 31, 1989.

# ANNIE WEBB BLANTON
## August 19, 1870 - October 2, 1945

Annie Webb Blanton, the first woman elected as president of the Texas State Teachers Association and as state superintendent of public instruction, had to overcome many obstacles in her career. She had to work twice as hard as a man to achieve her goals. Everything she did was questioned because she was a woman. But her determination for the right to hold those offices broke the gender barrier for women across the state of Texas.

**Political Activists**

Annie Blanton came from a family of political activists. Her ancestors fought in the American Revolution, the Civil War, and the Texas Revolution. Annie's parents, Thomas Lindsay and Eugenia Webb Blanton, did not fight in wars, but they carried on the family ideals. They taught their children that they had a personal duty to contribute to society. They believed education, and religion to a lesser degree, was the central foundation for such contributions. They also believed in a woman's responsibility to family and home duties.

Annie and her twin sister Fannie, born on August 19, 1870, were the second and third children of seven

9

*Annie Webb Blanton*
— Courtesy Texas State Teachers Association

to be born to the Blantons. May was two years older than the twins, who were followed by three brothers and one sister. Although the Blantons were not wealthy, they sent their children to a private school.

*". . . while I had the friendly help of many good men, there was always a faction of narrow prejudices who opposed everything that I attempted, not because there was no merit in what I was seeking, but because of the fact that the one initiating it was a woman . . ."*
— Annie Webb Blanton

Texas education was in a state of transition in the 1870s. The Reconstruction battles over public education were not yet solved. It was a common practice for children to attend private schools. A free public school system was not started until 1877. The schools were racially segregated for children aged eight to fourteen.

**Family Tragedy**

Annie was moved to a public school, but a series of tragedies changed educational plans for her and her sisters. The day after her youngest brother Eugene was born in 1879, her thirty-seven-year-old mother died of complications from childbirth. Her grief-stricken father moved his seven children, ranging in age from infant to eleven-year-old May, to LaGrange where his own mother lived.

May, Fannie, and Annie acted as substitute mothers to the younger children. The girls matured quickly as they accepted their duties in caring for their siblings. Annie's interest was primarily in reading to them. Her responsibilities increased in 1885 when her twin, Fannie, died of a childhood disease. Fifteen-year-old Annie was heartbroken, but she continued her education.

Annie graduated from LaGrange High School in 1887, not quite seventeen years old. She wanted to enroll at the University of Texas, but once again her plans changed because of family responsibility. May married and moved to Austin. That left Annie as the oldest child at home. She could not leave her family as well as become a financial burden on her father. She needed to become financially independent and help her younger siblings.

**A Teacher**

In 1887 a college degree was not required for teachers. Annie applied for and accepted a teaching job in rural Fayette County, about twenty miles from her home. The one-room, one-teacher school in Pine Springs welcomed the enthusiastic teenager.

Blanton boarded with a farm family near the school. She had several marriage proposals from students who were near her own age, but she always declined. Although she missed her family and often was tempted to return home, she was determined to help her family by beginning her career. Another family tragedy, however, caused her to resign after one year.

12

Her father died in 1888, leaving the family in a state of confusion. Financial matters worsened for the children. Now Annie was responsible for her family. She decided to move her siblings and her paternal grandmother to Austin. Annie's maternal grandfather and her sister May lived there, and the family could be together. Also, it was where the University of Texas was located.

## Head of the Household

When Annie settled her family in Austin, she started looking for a teaching job. She passed the qualifying exam required by Austin public schools and was hired to teach at East Austin Elementary. Always in the back of her mind was her wish to attend college. Only two percent of the nation's women between the ages of eighteen and twenty attended college in 1890. The majority of society feared that higher education would distract women from becoming wives and mothers. Only the most dedicated and determined women went to college. Annie Blanton possessed both the desire and the determination.

In 1892 she enrolled at the University of Texas to fulfill her dream of a college education. It took her several years of attending night school and summer classes to graduate in 1899. Her life was devoted to teaching, raising her siblings, and studying at the same time. She later said of those difficult years, "As I taught during the time of my undergraduate work, I had no leisure for participation in social activities." Those years set the pattern for the rest of her life.

Blanton was unlike most of the women teachers. While teaching was a socially acceptable profession for single women, she did not see it as a dead end. She saw opportunity for advancement. It was not a stopping off place until she was married. She wanted a career that was both self-satisfying and made a social contribution. By 1901 Blanton's siblings were on their way to becoming independent. She was ready to move on.

**Career Advancement**

In 1902 Annie Blanton joined the faculty at North Texas State Normal College (now North Texas State University). The normal school was defined as "neither a college nor a university . . . its purpose to be 'for the special training of teachers.'" She had joined in the highest ranks of education in Texas. The average age of the students was twenty, and most of them had not graduated from high school. Blanton expected them to perform by her high standards.

From her first teaching experience in Pine Springs, Blanton saw many differences between male and female teachers. Men got all of the promotions regardless of a woman's capabilities. Men were paid more than women and often had fewer duties. White men were paid more than white women, who were paid more than black men. Black female teachers were at the bottom of the pay scale.

By 1916, Blanton was ready to try to change those differences. She spoke to the most important teachers' organization in the state—the Texas State Teachers Association (TSTA). She expressed her desire to see women teachers have an opportunity to reach greater professional growth. The inequities between qualified men and women should stop, she said. When Blanton left the

14

meeting, she found herself president-elect of the association. She was the first woman to be elected to that position and the first woman to become president of the association. Blanton set a leadership standard that followed her for the rest of her life.

## State Superintendent

Blanton was a popular president of the TSTA. Teachers all over the state urged her to run for state superintendent of public instruction in Texas. The 1918 race for the office was highly controversial. For the first time in the history of the state, a woman was challenging male candidates for the office. She was frightening to her opponents because she was an excellent speaker, and people all over the state came to hear her.

There was a bitter two-month campaign. Her male opponents incorrectly reported that she had been divorced and was an atheist. They also said she was barred from serving on the State Textbook Board. One candidate, W. F. Doughty, said Blanton was being used by others and that she did not have a chance of winning.

Blanton answered the charges clearly and concisely. She told her audiences that she was single and a Christian. She explained that she was disqualified from serving as a member of the Textbook Board because she had written several textbooks used in the public schools. Blanton told voters that if Doughty "had carried his candidacy to the Creator in prayer as earnestly as I have, he would not have been endorsed by the breweries."

Blanton won the election and served two terms in office. Her goals for the department were ambitious and progressive. She worked toward expanding the department, improving rural schools, giving equal recognition to men and women employees, raising the scholastic and professional requirements of teachers, and working for pay raises for teachers. She worked to see that black children received funding and encouraged the teaching of English to Spanish-speaking children. She hired women in positions of leadership and encouraged them to help place other female members on school boards.

**Advanced Degree**

Blanton retired from public office in 1922 and returned to the University of Texas to complete her master's degree. She taught at the University of Texas until 1926, when she went to Cornell University to work on her doctorate. In 1927 she received her Ph.D. and returned to the University of Texas as an associate professor.

Although Blanton did not run for state office again, she remained active in the Democratic party. Continuing her work for the advancement of educational legislation, she served three terms as vice-president of the National Education Association and was an active member of the National Council on Education.

In 1929 Blanton formed a professional society for women educators, first named Kappa Gamma Delta and then changed to Delta Kappa Gamma. The founders worked to stop discrimination that existed toward women in the education field by giving scholarships to help outstanding female leaders pursue graduate studies. Thousands of women educators all over the world have been given financial support to continue graduate studies.

16

By 1939 Blanton requested part-time status at the university so she could devote more time to Delta Kappa Gamma. In September 1945 she resigned from the university because of ill health. She died on October 2, 1945.

Annie Webb Blanton fulfilled not only her dreams, but also a prophecy that one newspaper editor made about her: "She is a woman that time will call great."

*Mary Eleanor Brackenridge*

18

# MARY ELEANOR BRACKENRIDGE
## March 7, 1837 - February 14, 1924

A TEXAS FIRST
AS A
BUSINESS-
WOMAN AND
WOMEN'S
CLUB
FOUNDER

Mary Eleanor Brackenridge was the first woman in the United States to serve on the board of directors of a bank. She fought for education and improved care for women and children. In founding the Women's Club, she organized women to work for a higher purpose than socializing. She was one of three females to be appointed to serve on a college board in Texas. Although unmarried herself, she influenced legislation regarding married women's property rights.

**Social Activists**

Eleanor Brackenridge came from a long line of social activists. Her grandfather, John Brackenridge, set the standards for the family. Reverend Brackenridge was a First Presbyterian minister of Washington City (now Washington, D.C.). He believed in the advancement of Presbyterianism and education and thought the two went together.

The Reverend Brackenridge and his wife Eleanor named their first two sons for Presidents James Madison and John Adams, members of their congregation. Their other sons were also named after presidents of the United States. All of their children were educated to become doctors, lawyers, or ministers. John Adams, the

19

second son and father of Mary Eleanor, studied religion, medicine, and law. He practiced law in Indiana and served in the state legislature.

*"Women's clubs are no longer amusing; they are the solemn rising of the good women of the land who organize to stand together as a unit to work for higher purposes."*
—Mary Eleanor Brackenridge

In 1829 John Adams Brackenridge married Isabella Helena McCullough in Boonville, Indiana. They lived in a large house on one hundred acres of land. All eight of their children were born in the house. Brackenridge was prosperous and well respected. He and his wife had a good life, but they also had sadness. Two of their daughters died at a very early age, leaving four sons and two daughters. Brackenridge's poor health caused the family to move to Texana, Texas, where he established the Brackenridge Plantation in the mid-1850s.

The oldest daughter and third child born to the Brackenridges was Mary Eleanor, born on March 7, 1838, in Boonville, Indiana. Her father's wealth provided her the best education of that time. She attended and graduated from Anderson Female Seminary at New Albany, Indiana. After her graduation in 1855, she traveled to Texas to be with her family.

## A Tragic Romance

According to family history, shortly after her arrival in Texas, Eleanor fell in love with a young man of quality and character, but who was also very poor. Her mother refused to allow them to marry. The young man went away to make a fortune so he would be acceptable for Eleanor to marry. After three years he returned with a fortune, but he was desperately ill with tuberculosis. Eleanor's mother said that marriage was out of the question. The young man died a year later and left Eleanor his fortune, but her mother did not allow Eleanor to accept any of the money. It was given instead to the young man's brother and sister, who needed it. Eleanor never again considered dating or marriage. Until her death, she visited his grave every Christmas and on his birthday.

Eleanor Brackenridge was a religious person and was very serious about changing women's role in society. She could have spent her days like other young society ladies whose lives were filled with parties, teas, and gossip, but she threw herself into helping others. Her life was governed by her childhood motto: "I want to make the world better and therefore happier for all, not just for Eleanor."

## A Traveling Librarian

Eleanor and her father established the first Presbyterian church in Jackson County, Texas, in 1855. They were charter members and Mr. Brackenridge served as one of the ruling elders. Among the congregation Miss Brackenridge saw country women who were uneducated because they had no opportunity to attend schools. She taught girls to read and write and collected books, magazines, and newspapers. She operated the first mobile library from a carriage loaded with reading materials.

Traveling the countryside with her library, she noticed the suffering and hardships of country people without medical aid. She began to study basic medicine, collected medicines, and took a nurse with her to help the sick. Her efforts to promote health education had to be put aside with the beginning of the Civil War in 1861.

Mr. Brackenridge, a staunch Union supporter, was very ill and was heartbroken by a division in his family caused by the Civil War. His sons John Thomas, James Madison, and John Robert joined the Confederacy. Another son, George Washington, joined the Union. Mr. Brackenridge died on December 22, 1862, with his wife and two daughters at his bedside.

## San Antonio

Eleanor lived with her mother and younger sister Lenora on the plantation for the duration of the war. After the war, George W. Brackenridge established a home in San Antonio, and Miss Brackenridge and her mother moved there in 1866. George Brackenridge was known for his ability to raise large sums of money and for being a friend of education. He not only encouraged his sister in her efforts to promote education for women, but also gave her financial assistance. She used her own money for many programs, but his wealth was greater than hers and had far-reaching effects on higher education.

Eleanor was an organizer. When she first moved to San Antonio, she became involved in the building of the Madison Square Presbyterian Church as one of the char-

22

ter members. Mr. Brackenridge was the first trustee of the church and helped financially with the building although he never attended church.

## Women's Clubs

In 1898 she organized Texas' first department club —Texas Women's Club—and was president of the San Antonio Women's Club for seven years. The club's motto was "Unity is our strength." The club studied laws affecting women and children. Through its influence, public schools added industrial training, and city hall hired a police matron and probation officer. Also, sanitary drinking fountains were mandated in all public schools. Eleanor Brackenridge additionally began the Texas Congress of Mothers, which is now known as the PTA (Parent Teachers Association).

Both Mr. Brackenridge and Miss Brackenridge were generous in establishing schools for all classes of people. Mr. Brackenridge helped found the University of Texas and Eleanor helped with Texas Woman's University (then called Texas Industrial Institute and College for the Education of the White Girls of the State of Texas in Arts and Sciences). She was one of the first three Texas women to be appointed to serve on the college board in 1903.

It took ten years of hard work by the Woman's Christian Temperance Union to establish the Texas Industrial Institute and College. Legislators who opposed the school said that "instinct will make a woman a perfect housekeeper, a model wife, a wise mother." Others said that if "girls were taught to earn a living, they would cease getting married and within fifty years there wouldn't be a baby born in the state." Helen Stoddard, Eleanor Brackenridge, and Mrs. Cone Johnson, three educated women elected to the first board of regents, proved them wrong.

## Education for All

Eleanor Brackenridge gave equally to the white and black races. She established and financed a black kindergarten, and gave equal sums of money to both the white and black Young Woman's Christian Association of San Antonio. Eleanor also established a scholarship fund for three girls through the Women's Club of San Antonio. No record was kept of the number of scholarships she gave to both boys and girls because she did not want personal recognition for her good deeds.

Miss Brackenridge introduced the idea of home economics and manual training to be taught in the San Antonio public schools. The classes began with women in the Women's Club teaching cooking and sewing in their homes. She purchased sewing machines, stoves, and other equipment which made it possible for students to be trained in homemaking. The first home economics classes in the San Antonio public school system were opened in 1910. Miss Brackenridge believed home economics should be an elective subject to be taken by all girls. She gave scholarships to girls in homemaking classes if they wanted to attend the College of Industrial Arts.

Miss Brackenridge believed a child's environment was important to his or her development. Mr. Brackenridge shared her opinion and donated parks to the city. The largest was a two-hundred-acre site named Brackenridge Park. The park was designated for exclusive park

24

purposes and has been described as "one of the most beautiful [parks] in the south." It was a haven for women and children where they could play and feel safe.

## Juvenile Delinquency

One of Miss Brackenridge's concerns was juvenile delinquency. She introduced a plan to the Women's Club to establish a juvenile training school, a detention home for undisciplined young men. The club raised the funds to build the Southwestern Juvenile Training School on city property on the outskirts of town. Miss Brackenridge was the only woman to serve on its board of control from its beginning until the board was no longer needed.

By 1909 Miss Brackenridge was urging that a home be established for delinquent girls. Alexander Joske, the Brackenridges' friend, established the first home for delinquent girls, called Joske's Home for Girls (now known as the Bexar County School for Girls). Miss Brackenridge felt that there would be less delinquency if women were better educated and felt they had equal rights. She favored laws pertaining to the welfare of women and children, and led club women to write city, state, and national representatives for assistance in passing laws to benefit women. Eleanor urged them to become aware of their surroundings and to crusade for a cleaner and healthier community. In 1907 she became the first woman to serve on the Board of Health and be elected as first vice-president of the Health Protective Association.

## A Leader and Contributor

In 1913 Miss Brackenridge was elected president of the Texas Woman Suffrage Association. The movement had lain dormant since 1905. Within a year there were twenty-one local chapters and 2,500 members. She served one term and stayed active until women won the right to vote in primary elections. She was the first woman to register to vote in Bexar County in 1918.

Eleanor Brackenridge was the first woman in the United States to become a bank director, a position she held for more than thirty years. She used her business ability to develop sound principles in educating women and children. Her own wealth was the resource for scholarships, clubs, and educational institutions. She supported the arts as an important part of human existence and financed public parks for San Antonians. Although she was very wealthy, Miss Brackenridge did not live to make money. Her joy in life came from putting her money to use for education, women's welfare, and children.

Until her death on February 14, 1924, in her home named Fern Ridge, she lived as she taught: "Learn to do something; when every woman is a good woman, the world will be right."

# LINDA CHAVEZ-THOMPSON
## August 3, 1944 -

**A TEXAS FIRST IN THE LABOR MOVEMENT**

Linda Chavez-Thompson is the highest ranking woman or person of color in the labor movement. She is the third ranking member of the American Federation of Labor and Congress of Industrial Organizations (AFL-CIO). She was the only American of Mexican descent appointed by President Bill Clinton to serve on the president's Initiative on Race. She was the international vice-president of the American Federation of State, County, and Municipal Employees.

## A Name Change

Lydia Chavez went to her first day of school with great excitement. The small six-year-old wanted to learn to read and write and to speak English like her two older sisters. She was not afraid even though she spoke only Spanish. She returned home at the end of her first day in first grade with a new name. The Anglo teacher had changed her name to Linda.

She did not understand why the teacher insisted on calling her Linda. Her parents had taught her to respect and obey authority, and she was too shy to insist that the teacher call her by Lydia, her real name. Children of Mexican descent at the school lived mostly on farms around

*Linda Chavez-Thompson*
—Courtesy Linda Chavez-Thompson

Lorenzo. They were treated like second-class citizens. They were not allowed to have a voice of their own.

Lydia (Linda) Chavez was born on August 3, 1944, in Lorenzo, Texas, near Lubbock. Her parents, Felipe and Genoveva Chavez, were first-generation Americans. Her grandparents had moved to Texas during the Mexican Revolution at the Mexican government's request. Her grandfather was as politically active as an American of Mexican descent could be at the time. He had become an American citizen when he moved to Texas and owned a farm near Lorenzo.

*"I'm a woman and I'm tan and I'm from Texas. I represent the America that organized labor has tended to overlook."*
—Linda Chavez-Thompson

### A Sharecropper's Daughter

Linda's father, Felipe Chavez, was a cotton sharecropper. A landowner furnished a house for the family, farm equipment to use, and land for Chavez to raise cotton. In return Chavez was paid a small salary based on the amount of money made on the cotton crop. Mrs. Chavez and the children chopped cotton all summer to help out in the fields.

Mr. Chavez was very proud of his heritage. When it was popular for Americans of Mexican descent to be called "Chicanos," he would not allow the term to be used in his house. He thought it was derogatory, a way of showing a low opinion of Americans of Mexican descent. He taught his children to take pride in their heritage, but he would not challenge white authority.

Lydia did not challenge her teacher in first grade. She became known by two different names. She was Linda at school and Lydia at home and in the cotton field. She was always mature for her age although she was small in size. There were two older sisters, Maria and Martina, who were less than a year apart. Mrs. Chavez was very ill when she was pregnant with Martina. The grandparents took Maria until Mrs. Chavez was well again. By the time she was able to care for the two small girls, the grandparents had become so attached to Maria they did not want to give her up. Maria continued to live with them. Linda was the fourth girl to be born to Mr. and Mrs. Chavez. The third daughter died in infancy.

Maria and Martina were five and six years old when Linda was born. Maria came often to play with Martina and Linda. Linda tried to do everything they did. Martina did not want Linda with her and Maria when they played or went somewhere. Martina knew what a little pest she could be, but Maria was more tolerant. "Don't turn those little cow eyes on me," Martina told her. "It won't work on me." But it always worked on Maria, and Linda generally got her way.


**Introduction to Racism**

Linda was around ten years old when she came in direct contact with racism. She was good friends with three Anglo girls in her class. They designed and drew clothes to share with each other. One day Linda had some new drawings to show her friends, but the girls ignored her at recess and at lunch. She could not understand why they were avoiding her until one of the girls told her, "My mama says I can't play with you anymore because you are a Mexican." She did not understand why they made "Mexican" sound like a dirty word. Linda was very hurt by their rejection. She cried when the girls turned and walked away. They never played with her again.

There were many migrant workers who came through West Texas during cotton picking season. The migrant children were treated worse than the children of residents of Mexican descent. The migrant children took lunches in bags or wrappers because they could not afford to buy school lunches. Children made fun of their potato and egg tacos. When a cousin of Felipe Chavez came through as a migrant worker, his daughter went to school with the Chavez children. Linda was ashamed of her and would not admit that she was related to her. Those experiences later influenced Linda in her choice of a profession.

Through the years Victor, San Juana ( Janie), Philip, Jr., Antonio, and Amy were added to the family. Mrs. Chavez, Martina, and Linda worked in the cotton fields hoeing cotton with Mr. Chavez from the time school was out until school began again in the fall. When they finished their own fields, Mr. Chavez hired out the family to hoe in other fields. They had a reputation for being good workers, so they always had work to do. As the smaller children got old enough, they became workers too.

## A Young Negotiator

Linda decided to act as a spokesperson and talk to her dad about allowing her mother to stay home with the small children. It was her first labor-bargaining job. Mrs. Chavez got up earlier than anyone else in the household. She prepared breakfast, dressed the small children, and prepared lunch to take to the field before leaving to work all day. When she came home, she had to prepare dinner for the large family. The children thought it was unfair that their mother had to work longer hours than anyone else. After Linda's argument, their mother never worked in the fields again.

Linda was always the one to talk to her father about changes. She always respected him but was willing to argue with him. When he said, "I'll think about it," she knew he would agree to her request. Still, her father's rules were different for the girls than for the boys. The girls were never allowed to go anywhere unless they were chaperoned. They were not allowed to date and had to meet their boyfriends at parties or dances. The boys were given more freedom.

## A High School Dropout

Linda had finished her freshman year in high school when her father told her she could not go back to school in the fall. She had just had her sixteenth birthday and was looking forward to her sophomore year. Mr. Chavez explained that he could not afford to have more than four children in school at the same time on his thirty-dollar-a-week salary. It was more important for the boys to get an education than for the girls, who would just get married, he reasoned.

Linda cried and begged her father to change his mind. Her best friend's mother offered to let Linda live with them through the week and pay Linda's expenses. Linda could come home on the weekends to help out with the family. But her father would not allow her to do it. A young girl did not leave home nor did the Chavez family accept charity.

When the school bus passed the cotton field on the first day of school, Linda could not stop crying. She cried for two weeks but finally accepted that she was not going to school. That did not keep her from learning. She read every book that her siblings brought home and had them check out books from the library. She taught herself to read Spanish by reading her father's magazines.

## From Field Work to Housework

Linda and Martina pulled cotton at the end of the rows where the cotton-stripping machine turned around. After they finished that they worked with migrant workers picking cotton. When Linda could not work in the fields, she was taught to clean houses. The wife of the landowner where they lived paid Linda housekeeping wages while she taught her how to clean house. Linda became so good at it that soon she was cleaning other people's houses five days a week. She sometimes made as much as ten dollars a day.

When she was nineteen, she went to work for a lawyer's family in Lubbock. The family had six children with the seventh on the way. Mr. Chavez took Linda to Lubbock on Sunday night and picked her up on Friday evening. She spent the rest of the week as a full-time housekeeper. She was not allowed to date, but living in Lubbock gave her freedom that she did not have at home.

She began dating a man ten years older that she had known when she lived at home. He asked her father for her hand in marriage. Mr. Chavez said the decision was up to Linda. They were married and moved to Lubbock.

## Labor Unions

Linda's goal was to become a clerk in a department store instead of cleaning houses. Her daughter, Maricela Ramirez, was born in 1965, but Linda continued to work. In December 1967 her uncle recommended her for a job with the local labor union office. About sixty percent of their members were Spanish speaking and they needed a bilingual secretary in the office. She accepted the job with the understanding that she could type. She did not tell the business manager of the office that she typed with two fingers. Linda began the job with a "ten pound knot in her stomach." She had no idea what it meant to be a secretary and knew even less about a labor union.

It did not take her long to become popular with the Laborers' International Union members. She organized the office and began writing letters in Spanish to non-English readers. A worker in the print shop next door to the office taught her how to work the mimeograph machine to make copies of notices for circulation. She set up a system for notifying members about jobs. Linda soon realized that organized laborers made a much better salary than those who had no representation. The labor movement became the focus of her professional life. Her career in issues of public employment began because Lubbock city employees had no one to represent them.

She became the union members' representative, writing grievances for them and counseling them about their options.

## San Antonio to Washington, D.C.

After she and her husband moved to San Antonio, their son, Pedro Javier Ramirez, was born in 1976. Then, after more than twenty years of marriage, the couple divorced. In 1985 she married Robert Thompson, a long-time local union president in San Antonio. Thompson died of cancer in 1993.

From secretary of the Laborers' International Union in Lubbock, Chavez-Thompson rose quickly through the ranks. In 1971 she became an International Union representative of the American Federation of State, County, and Municipal Employees (AFSCME). She served in several positions with the San Antonio Local and Texas Council of AFSCME from 1973 through 1995, and was responsible for advancing legislative, political action, and education programs. From June 1988 through June 1996, she was an international vice-president of AFSCME. She directed the union's efforts in Arizona, Colorado, Nevada, New Mexico, Oklahoma, Texas, and Utah, a seven-state district that is widely recognized as unfriendly toward labor. Her reputation grew nationwide.

Although Chavez-Thompson rose in positions never held by a woman or Latino, acceptance did not come easily. "It was almost like I had to prove myself again and again," she said. When she was running for her current position as executive vice-president of AFL-CIO, the opposing campaign called her a "token" because she was a woman and a Mexican-American. Her response to the accusation was, "Anyone will tell you, Linda won't be a token for [anybody]."

**Achievements**

Chavez-Thompson has helped diversify AFL-CIO to include more women and women's issues. She believes that "each woman is born with certain talents. She should never be afraid to develop that inner self. Education is important but should not be used as an excuse not to develop that inner self. Women face many obstacles— lack of education, their own cultures, parents' ideas of what is best for them. They must consider all of those things but not let them stand in the way of becoming the best they can at whatever they set as their goals."

Linda Chavez-Thompson is still known by family as Lydia, but Linda has been her professional name for so long that she changed all official records to read "Lydia (Linda) Chavez-Thompson." Her current goal is not to be remembered as the highest-ranking woman in the AFL-CIO, but just to be the first of many. She hopes to change racial attitudes so that no child will go to school with one name and come home with another. Her success will help determine that her grandchildren, Jose Felipe and Lydia, will never face the problems their grandmother faced.

# SUE MARGARET "MAGGIE" COUSINS
## January 26, 1905 - July 30, 1996

Nationally known as "Maggie," Sue Margaret Cousins devoted her life to writing and writers. She became an editor of a Texas magazine when it was unheard of for a woman to fill that position in publishing. When she was refused a job as editor in New York, she moved to a publishing house that would hire her in that capacity. In a career spanning more than seventy-five years, she wrote short stories, nonfiction articles, biographies, children's books, novels, poems, and inspirational essays in addition to editing thousands of manuscripts.

### A Native Texan

Maggie Cousins was born in a big farm house surrounded by ranches on January 26, 1905, near Munday, Texas. The summers were burning hot and the winters were freezing cold. There were many storms and tornadoes in the spring months. The Cousins family had a storm cellar where they stayed during the storms that often came suddenly in the night. Mrs. Cousins was afraid the house would fall on the dugout, so Mr. Cousins put in two doors—one in the front and one in the back. Although the storms were frightening for the adults, Maggie was excited by the thunder, lightning, and wind.

*Sue Margaret "Maggie" Cousins*
—Courtesy Corona Publishing Company,
San Antonio, Texas

Maggie did not know any children her age, but she had two teenage aunts who spoiled her. She often ran away to her grandmother's house, which was across the pasture. Her father did not like for her to run away. When he came for her, he made her walk back home. She got stickers in her feet and begged to be carried. "You walked over here, you can walk home," he told her.

Maggie was very imaginative and created her own entertainment. She had an imaginary horse for a playmate. When she refused to admit it was just a fantasy, her parents allowed the horse to eat at the table with them. They even put a small pile of oats on the table for the horse to eat during mealtimes. After her brother was born, "It just left me," she recalled. "It just flew off with wings."

> *"I was trained to be an editor and I expected to be one. But when the job as editor opened up, the chairman of the board said, 'I'll never give the job to a woman.' I resigned that day."*
> —Sue Margaret Cousins

### An Early Reader

Maggie taught herself to read by the time she was four years old. She learned the alphabet from everyday products like Bon Ami soap and Calumet baking powder. Her parents read to her and she watched them read in the evenings. Her mother, Sue Margaret Reeves Cousins, subscribed to home-service magazines like *Ladies' Home*

*Journal, Good Housekeeping,* and *McCall's.* Maggie believed that being introduced to those magazines at an early age led her to a career in writing and editing for women's magazines.

Cousins' father, Walter Henry Cousins, was also a major influence on her literary career. He became a registered pharmacist in 1902 and was the first pharmacist in Munday. He wrote humorous stories, essays, and cowboy verse for several magazines. He also shared his love of great literature with his children by reading to them from the works of Charles Dickens, Edgar Allan Poe, O. Henry, and others. Books were very expensive, but Maggie always wanted them for Christmas. Her favorite gift was *A Child's Garden of Verses* by Robert Louis Stevenson. She memorized the book and dreamed of going to London, the setting of the book.

**A Young Writer**

When Cousins was ten, her father bought the *Southern Pharmaceutical Journal* and the family moved to Dallas. Maggie was in the fourth grade and had only boys as playmates. One day they went bug-hunting in Mr. Nicholson's garden. The boys cut a bunch of beautiful red tulips for Maggie because she was the only girl. She ran home to show her mother. When her mother learned where she got them, she placed them in vases all over the house. Every time anyone asked where the tulips came from, Mrs. Cousins said, "Margaret stole them." She never stole flowers again.

Maggie had started writing stories and verse before the family moved to Dallas. At age twelve she sold her first poem to *Motion Picture Magazine*. She was the class poet in high school and wrote for school publications. She gave credit to her teachers at Bryan Street High School in Dallas for her background in literature, American history, and journalism.

Cousins chose the University of Texas at Austin for her college education because of its journalism school. She joined Theta Sigma Phi, a society for female journalists, and worked on the staffs of the *Texas Ranger* and *Longhorn Magazine*. During that time she became the first woman issue editor (one night each week) for the *Daily Texan*.

After graduating from the University of Texas in 1926, Cousins worked for ten years for her father on the *Southern Pharmaceutical Journal*. She helped with the secretarial work, learned to set Linotype, solicited stories, and wrote editorials and feature articles. When she and her father disagreed on some of the pieces she wrote, she submitted the manuscripts to other pharmaceutical publications. Much to her surprise and her father's embarrassment, New York editors began to take an interest in her writing.

In the ten years she worked for her father, she worked her way up to editor of the magazine, a position unheard of for a woman. She continued to write verse and articles for other publications. In 1936, editor Herbert R. Mayes offered Cousins a job on the staff of *American Druggist*. Cousins refused the offer because she felt the magazine was in competition with her father's publication. She told Mayes that her real ambition was to work on a service magazine for women.

**New York Calls**

When Mayes became editor of *Pictorial Review* in 1937, he asked Cousins to become his associate editor. *Pictorial Review* was in financial trouble and closed after two years. In 1939 Mayes went to work for *Good Housekeeping*. Cousins moved to the general promotion department of Hearst Magazines, which owned *Good Housekeeping,* among many other publications. She wrote copy, seasonal features and essays, as well as fiction that appeared regularly.

By 1942 she was writing less poetry and more fiction. Her writing took another turn when she began ghostwriting, which she continued to do occasionally for many years. That was also the year she became associate editor at *Good Housekeeping*. Many of her stories were published in the magazine. Although she was a popular editor and writer, her name as managing editor did not appear on the staff listing (masthead) of the magazine until September 1945.

**A Children's Author**

In 1952 Bennett Cerf, editor at Random House Publishers, asked Cousins to write a biography of Benjamin Franklin for children. She wrote *Ben Franklin of Old Philadelphia* (1952). The book was published in several languages and was last published in the United States in 1987. Cousins' second juvenile book, *We were there at the Alamo* (1958), was reprinted under the title *The Boy in the Alamo* in 1983 by Corona Press. Her third book for children, *The Story of Thomas Alva Edison,* was published in 1965.

Cousins wrote so many stories for so many publications that she used three pseudonyms: Mary Parrish, Avery Johns, and William Masters. Her agent, Harold Matson, sold several of her short stories to television, and a novelette, "The Life of Lucy Gallant," was made into a movie.

*Good Housekeeping* broke all records in circulation and advertising, but Mayes had a dispute with the executive vice-president of Hearst and was fired as editor. He was offered the position of editor of *McCall's* and took it with the understanding that he had absolute control. Cousins moved to *McCall's* with him as managing editor. She continued to send stories to other magazines while she wrote for *McCall's,* and she was called upon to edit celebrity columns such as those by Clare Boothe Luce and Eleanor Roosevelt.

## A Job Dispute

When Mayes became president and chief executive officer of the McCall's Corporation in 1961, he wanted Cousins to learn the business side of publishing. Cousins did not want to leave her position in editing and writing. She felt she should be moved up to chief editor. When the president of the board said that a woman would never hold that position, Cousins quit that day. John Mack Carter then took the editorship of *McCall's.*

Cousins went to Doubleday Publishers as senior editor. She worked on many of Doubleday's series. She corresponded with editors, authors, and illustrators. She made speeches on behalf of Doubleday and worked on promotion and publicity committees. When Doubleday told her she had to retire at the age of sixty-five, she was very angry. She was not ready to retire.

Cousins looked for another job and became a special editor with Holt, Rinehart and Winston. She edited the autobiographies of President and Mrs. Lyndon Baines Johnson. *A White House Diary* by Mrs. Johnson was published in 1970, and *The Vantage Point* by President Johnson was published in 1971.

In 1971 John Mack Carter asked Cousins to take the position of book editor at *Ladies' Home Journal*. She had worked as book editor there for two years when she fell down on the street during a noon break. When she was diagnosed as having rheumatoid arthritis, she decided to retire. Cousins had never married and her relatives were widespread. She chose to retire in San Antonio, because she had been there as a child and loved it. But she never lost touch with writers and the publishing business.

## A Publishing Pioneer

Maggie Cousins began her career in an era when women were not accepted in positions of authority in the publishing world. She did not let that stop her from competing in a man's world. She stood by her principles and gained recognition during a time when women were expected to be housewives and mothers. She was not only an editor, but a friend to all writers with whom she came in contact. She was kind, considerate, helpful, patient, and hardworking. Over a period of seventy-five years, Cousins wrote nearly two hundred stories and essays that were published in the United States and foreign magazines while establishing her reputation as an editor.

"Of all the writers who penned the fiction that filled this country's women's magazines fifty years ago, few were more prolific than Margaret Cousins. And none more warmly received by readers or more affectionately remembered by colleagues," wrote John Mack Carter, former editor-in-Chief of *Good Housekeeping*.

Cousins once said, "I think if you don't plan to have magic in your life, you won't have it. When I came to San Antonio, I decided to have an adventure every day. . . . I'll never get bored until I haven't got time to have an adventure." When Sue Margaret Cousins died on July 30, 1996, novelist Robert Flynn said, "I think for Maggie, death is another adventure." Herbert R. Mayes said of Cousins' career, "Editorially, there was nothing Miss Cousins couldn't and didn't do."

Maggie Cousins was a legend in her own lifetime. She set high standards for women to follow in the publishing world.

*Olive Ann Oatman Fairchild*
—Courtesy Red River Historical Museum,
Sherman, Texas

46

# OLIVE ANN OATMAN FAIRCHILD
## 1837 - 1903

Olive Ann Oatman was neither the first nor the last Indian captive. She was, however, the first to go on a lecture tour to promote a best-selling book about her five years living as an Indian captive. When she died in Sherman, Texas, she still had the tattoo on her chin which identified her as belonging to the Mohaves and protected her body after death, assuring her a peaceful eternity.

### A Short Childhood

Olive Ann Oatman was born in Illinois in September 1837. She was the third of seven children born to Royse and Mary Ann Sperry Oatman. The Oatmans lived on a farm near La Harpe, Illinois, when Lucy (1833) and Lorenzo (1836) were born. By the time Olive was born, Oatman had bought a mercantile business and moved from the farm to town. Oatman, along with many other businessmen, lost his money when the bank industry crashed in the late 1830s.

Oatman moved his family to Cumberland Valley, Pennsylvania, where he hoped to begin again. Three more children were added to the family: Mary Ann (1843), Royse, Jr. (1845), and another daughter known only as C. A. (1846). But Oatman's "love for the free life of the western prairies . . . drew him back" to a log cabin near Fulton, Illinois, in 1846. Their seventh child, a son, was born there.

Royse Oatman was an adventurer. He wanted to go west. The Oatman family joined a group of Brewsterites, a religious sect, who had left the main body of the Mormons led by Brigham Young and Joseph Smith. The sect's leader, James Collins Brewster, had experienced a divine prophecy which directed the group to establish a town called Basham at the mouth of the Colorado River in New Mexico Territory. "The Lord had directed it; it was their destiny."

> *"The facts connected with the history of my* Father's *family and my* Captivity *among the Indians passes all the material of a thrilling romance."*
> —Olive Ann Oatman

Royse Oatman was not one to question God's orders. Besides, he was a wanderer and was ready to explore the West. Mrs. Oatman, pregnant with her eighth child, calmly began to pack for the trip. Oatman sold his farm for $1,500, loaded his wife and children and provisions for eighteen months in two wagons, and joined the party of Brewsterites at Independence, Missouri.

Olive, not quite thirteen, counted twenty wagons as they began their exodus to Basham on August 10, 1850. They were on the Santa Fe Trail, headed to their divine city. Olive was filled with excitement and fear. She wanted to explore new lands in the West. She was afraid because they were traveling in Indian territory.

## Santa Fe Trail

Olive's excitement overcame her fear as she made new friends. Each day offered something new and wonderful to explore. She and her friends ran and danced along the trail of the slow-moving wagons. In the evenings they joined the adults for worship and ended the day singing hymns of praise to God.

Gradually arguments began among the men in the party. Some wanted to stop where there were already settlers. Others wanted to continue to Basham on the Colorado River. Still others wanted to go to California, where gold was rumored to be in all the streams just waiting to be panned. The train divided when Brewster decided to establish a colony on Socorro Peak. Royse Oatman led eight wagons with twenty people toward California.

It was a dismal journey through the mountains of Arizona and New Mexico. Stock either died or was stolen by the Apaches. Some of the wagons and baggage had to be left behind because there were not enough teams to pull them. Water and food became scarce. There were signs of Indians on every trail.

Some of the settlers decided to stop in Tucson and go no farther. The Oatman, Wilder, and Kelley families went on to Pima Village, Arizona. By the time they reached Pima Village, their situation was worse than ever. While they rested at the village, Dr. John Lawrence LeConte arrived after crossing the Gila Trail. He was a distinguished entomologist who had been studying insects on the Gila River. He reported that he had seen no Indians for two hundred miles. The Wilders and Kelleys decided to stay at the village to replace their supplies before continuing their journey. But Oatman was a stubborn man. Against everyone's advice, he decided to take his family in one wagon and go on their own.

### A Solitary Journey

The Gila Trail was a difficult one to travel. The Oatmans frequently had to unload their wagon so the tired and hungry oxen could pull it to the top of a hill. On the eighth day of travel, the destitute family was met by Dr. LeConte on his way back to Fort Yuma. Oatman sent a message by LeConte asking for help for his family. Hope for help to come spurred the family on their westward journey. But unknown to them, Dr. LeConte and his guide were attacked by Indians and barely managed to escape with their lives. Dr. LeConte left a note pinned on the trail warning the Oatmans about hostile Indians in the area. Oatman either did not see the warning or ignored it as they pushed on toward Fort Yuma.

On February 15, 1851, their oxen bogged down in the mud in the middle of the Gila River. They spent a miserable night camped on a small sandbar. Olive, Lorenzo, and Lucy spent the night whispering about the dangers they might encounter. They talked about their carefree days of the past and their hopes for the future. But they always came back to the possibility of an Indian attack.

"I shall run," said Lucy.

"I will take a gun or a club and keep them off," declared Lorenzo. "I will fight and die fighting!"

"Well, there is one thing; I shall not be taken by those miserable brutes. I will fight as long as I can, and if I see that I am about to be taken, I will kill myself," exclaimed Olive. "I do not care to die, but it would be worse than death to me to be taken captive among them!"

When the sun sent its crimson rays over the dismal and solitude camp, Olive's father double-yoked the oxen and milk cows to pull the wagon from the bog. By pushing and pulling the wagon with the animals, the family reached the other side of the river. The weary Oatmans rested during the blistering heat of the overhead sun and began the steep incline to the ridge. At one point when they were struggling to reach the summit, Olive's father suddenly sank down on a rock near the wagon. "Mother, mother, in the name of God, I know something is going to happen!" he cried.

The summit of the ridge was a long, level tableland that stretched westward between two deep gorges. Olive and Lucy helped their mother prepare a few pieces of dried bread and bean soup for their supper. As the sun was setting and a full moon rising, Lorenzo saw Indians approaching from the trail they had just traveled.

**Tragedy Strikes**

Lorenzo quietly called his father's attention to the approaching band of Yavapais. Mr. Oatman turned crimson and then a deathlike paleness spread over his face as he looked in horror. He spoke to the Indians in Spanish

51

and invited them to sit. They demanded tobacco and he shared a pipe with them.

The Yavapais, dressed in wolfskins, asked for food. Oatman gave them a small amount and begged them to leave the rest so his family would not starve. The band withdrew a short distance and began speaking in their own tongue. "Suddenly as a clap of thunder from a clear sky, a deafening yell broke upon [the Oatmans], the Indians jumping into the air, and uttering the most frightful shrieks," brandished their weapons and attacked the defenseless family.

One of the braves jerked Olive out of the way before she was struck a death blow. She watched in horror as her family was massacred by the frenzied Yavapais. She was thrown on the ground and covered her head with her arms. When she looked again, she saw a sobbing Mary Ann standing by the wagon with her hands covering her face. A large Indian was standing over her. Olive fainted and fell to the earth. She awoke to Mary Ann's cries, "Mother, O mother! Olive, mother and father are killed, with all of our poor brothers and sisters." Olive begged her captors to kill her, but they just laughed and poked at her with their dirty feet.

The Yavapais took everything from the wagon and from the bodies of their victims that they could use. They used the cover of the wagon to carry their plunder and scattered the rest to the winds. Olive and Mary Ann were made to walk before the laughing band as they went down the hill the way they had come. Olive's worst nightmare had come true.

## Indian Captives

Olive and Mary Ann staggered along with bleeding feet and barely covered in rags. Thirteen-year-old Olive tried to comfort seven-year-old Mary Ann when Mary Ann's grief became uncontrollable. They prayed for death but lived in fear of being beaten. When Mary Ann collapsed on the trail and threats of a beating could not move her, an Indian picked her up and carried her on his back. When Olive's feet became so torn and sore that she could not walk, they made leather soles and tied them to her feet.

After three days and nights of constant walking over two hundred miles of rugged country, they arrived at the Yavapais' main camp. Olive and Mary Ann were put on top of a pile of brush and bark. Half-naked men, women, and children formed a circle around them. They ran, jumped, and danced to music made by clubs pounding on stones and the drawing of a string across bark. The dancers spat at the girls, threw dirt in their faces, and slapped at them to make them flinch. "That night was among the most horrible of our captivity. We thought they would kill us and hoped they would do so," Olive later said.

There were around three hundred members in the tribe. The women were the laborers and principal burden-bearers. During their captivity with the Yavapais, Olive said, "It was our lot to serve under these enslaved women, with a severity more intolerable than that to which they were subjected by their merciless lords."

After about a year the Yavapais traded Olive and Mary Ann to the Mohaves for two horses, three blankets, beads, and food. Once again they were marched over three hundred miles to their new home. Chief Espaniola, his wife, and Topeka, his seventeen-year-old daughter, took them in as their family. Each girl was given a blanket, food, a small plot for a garden, and seeds to plant. Both were tattooed with the tribal mark, the *Ki-e-chook*, five vertical lines from the lower lip to chin stained with blue dye. The tattoo marked them as property of the Mohaves and protected them from having to spend eternity in a rat's hole.

Olive and Mary Ann became victims of a drought in 1853 along with the other Mohaves. Many children and some adults died of starvation. Olive frantically tried to find blackbird eggs and seeds to feed Mary Ann. She watched her young, frail sister gradually starve to death. Olive was devastated and begged to be allowed to bury Mary Ann's body rather than follow the Mohave custom of burning the dead. Chief Espaniola's wife and daughter persuaded the chief to allow the burial. Olive stood over the grave and sang as many hymns as she could remember in her own language. She, too, wanted to die and thought she would gradually starve like her sister. The chief's wife ground up seed corn into gruel and fed it to her to keep her alive.

**Lorenzo**

Olive believed that she was the sole survivor of the Oatman family. Unknown to her, Lorenzo had survived the massacre and had spent five years searching for his sisters. He had written letters to newspapers, the governor, and Congress asking for help. Word had spread that he still believed his sisters were alive. He had never given up hope of finding them.

54

In February 1856, Francisco, a Yuma Indian, told Henry W. Grinnell, a civilian carpenter at Fort Yuma, that Olive was a captive of the Mohaves. Grinnell told the fort commander, who then sent Francisco with a letter demanding Olive's release. He also sent a ransom of four blankets, six pounds of white beads, some trinkets, and a white horse to insure her release.

The Mohaves debated long hours and the women shed many tears before Olive was freed to leave with Francisco. The break was not easy for Olive. She shed tears over Mary Ann's grave because she did not know what would happen to it after she left. She had become attached to Chief Espaniola's family and the rugged country around her village home.

When the rescue party arrived near Fort Yuma, Henry Grinnell met them with a borrowed dress for Olive to replace her bark skirt. She had forgotten a lot of the English language, but people were very kind and gentle with her. Lorenzo came to Fort Yuma as soon as he heard Olive was there. They did not recognize each other due to the changes in their lives over the past five years. Over an hour passed before they could talk because they were so overcome with emotion.

## Reentry Into Society

Olive and Lorenzo went to Los Angeles, California, where she was interviewed by newspapers. They also visited a cousin in Oregon, where they met the Reverend R. B. Stratton. Stratton became interested in the story of their lives and wrote *Captivity of the Oatman Girls*. The book became an immediate hit. Stratton then paid for

Olive and Lorenzo to attend the University of the Pacific in Santa Clara. By 1858, the book was a bestseller. Olive moved to New York with the Stratton family and decided to go on a lecture tour to promote the book. Lorenzo returned to Illinois, where he married and lived until his death in 1901.

Sometime in 1865 Olive met John Brandt Fairchild in New York. They fell in love and had a short courtship before their marriage in November of that year. Olive stopped lecturing about her captivity after her marriage. The Fairchilds lived in Detroit before moving to Sherman, Texas, in 1872. Mr. Fairchild opened the City Bank of Sherman, where he was president and chairman of the board.

Olive was shy and retiring but quietly did volunteer work for children in the community. The Fairchilds had no children of their own and adopted an infant daughter, Mary Elizabeth "Mamie," in March 1876. Olive was frequently seen around Sherman, recognizable by the dark veil she wore to cover her tattooed chin. She died of a heart attack on March 20, 1903, at the age of sixty-five.

It was not easy for a shy eighteen-year-old girl to stand before a curious audience to speak about her years as an Indian captive. Few captives spoke of their experiences and even fewer wrote about them. Because of an inner strength unknown to many, Olive Ann Oatman was able to do both.

# FRANCES TARLTON "SISSY" FARENTHOLD
## October 2, 1926 -

A TEXAS
FIRST
AS A
STATES-
WOMAN
AND
LAWYER

Frances Tarlton "Sissy" Farenthold attended law school when it was not easy for a woman to be accepted as a student or as a lawyer. She moved into politics because of her concern for the welfare of women and children. She served two terms as the only woman in the Texas House of Representatives. She was the first woman in United States history nominated for vice-president and voted upon at the Democratic National Convention.

**An Embarrassment**

Sissy Farenthold's many successes have not erased from her memory the anguish and embarrassment at not being able to read until she was nine years old. She lived in constant fear that she would be called upon to read aloud. When her father watched her "reading" a book upside down, her parents finally understood that she could not read.

Frances Tarlton, nicknamed "Sissy" by a brother, was born in Corpus Christi, Texas, on October 2, 1926. She was one of six children born to Benjamin Dudley and Catherine (Bluntzer) Tarlton. Her family had a tradition of public service and political involvement. Both her

*Frances Tarlton "Sissy" Farenthold*
—Courtesy Frances Tarlton Farenthold

father and grandfather Tarlton were lawyers and political activists. Her grandmother, Kate D. Bluntzer, was one of the first public schoolteachers in Corpus Christi. Lida Doughtery, an aunt, was the first woman superintendent of a county public school in Texas.

> *"A woman must choose a cause and work for it. Take risks. You can even make a fool of yourself, if you want, but take a risk."*
> — Frances Tarlton "Sissy" Farenthold

Coming from a large family of achievers put more pressure on Sissy. Even at a young age she realized how little she could do unless she could read and write. She attended a convent school from kindergarten until she was nine years old. Sissy was kept in the first grade because she could not read or write. The shy girl was humiliated to be passed by the younger children. Her first years of school were very painful for her.

**A New Beginning**

After her parents discovered that Sissy could not read, they put all of the children in Mrs. Boyd's private school. Mrs. Boyd had an unstructured, one-room school with twelve students, including the Tarlton children. It was a traumatic experience for Sissy, who was used to structure and discipline in the convent school. Mrs. Tarlton began teaching Sissy how to read. Each night

59

they sat on the side of the bed and practiced until Sissy understood the alphabet and what words meant. Mrs. Tarlton discovered that Sissy had dyslexia, a learning disorder causing Sissy to reverse letters and numbers.

As Sissy learned to read and write, her confidence grew and her teacher asked her to help the younger children with their reading. By the time she was in sixth grade, she had caught up with other children her age. She became an avid reader and read everything from Christopher Morley mysteries to the daily newspaper. "If you read newspapers as a kid by the time you are an adult, it is history," she said.

She attended Corpus Christi public schools during her middle school years, but graduated from the Hockaday School for girls in Dallas when she was sixteen. It was customary for young ladies of prominent families to make a debut into society. Sissy told her parents that she did not want to be a debutante because she "didn't like the exclusivity that debuts symbolize." She attended Vassar, an exclusive women's college in New York, at age sixteen because she "thought a woman could really get a serious education there." She chose not to join a college sorority. "I just couldn't visualize being serenaded under the window and that sort of thing," she later explained.

**Law and Marriage**

She graduated from Vassar in 1946 with a degree in political science and entered law school at the University of Texas at Austin. She was one of three women to graduate in 1949. Although she was an honor student, she was never interviewed by law firms for a job. After graduation she joined her father's law firm in Corpus Christi.

In 1950 Sissy married George Farenthold, who had earned a Bronze Star in World War II. The Farentholds had five children in four and a half years. Sissy devoted the 1950s to the traditional role of wife, mother, and volunteer. When her youngest son died in 1965, Farenthold applied for a job as director of the Nueces County Legal Aid Association. She was hired by the bar association to represent people who could not afford their own lawyers. Sissy quickly saw how Mexican-Americans and young women were discriminated against regarding salaries. Ninety percent of her cases were welfare related. She became known as a lawyer for the oppressed. "It was the most eye-opening experience of my life. . . . I don't think I would have gone into politics except for that," she said. As director of the association she learned about the inequities in the Texas welfare system.

## Politics

Farenthold had little political experience when Jake Jarmon, a law school colleague, suggested she run for a seat in the Texas legislature in 1968. She almost missed the filing deadline to become the first woman candidate to run in District 45, located on the lower Gulf Coast. When she decided to campaign for the seat, a veteran politician told her, "Lower your skirts and don't talk about your children."

Farenthold had not gotten over her childhood shyness and could not ask people to vote for her. The only place she passed out campaign cards was at the laundromat where she did her laundry. She sometimes stuck a card on the bulletin board. Finally, an experienced legislator told her husband that Farenthold had to get out and meet people. Sissy had to be recognized by voters, and the only way she could do that was to become visible. Time was running out. She had to act immediately.

That day, a Saturday, her husband drove her to the largest shopping mall in Corpus Christi. He gave her about twelve hundred campaign cards that had her name and slogan on them. Then he handed her a dime and said, "When you have handed all of these out, call me and I'll come to get you."

## Texas Legislator

Her campaign was poorly financed and she was not backed by her own Democratic party organization. Although Farenthold did not believe she would win, she eventually beat the Republican incumbent to become the only woman in the Texas House of Representatives from 1968 to 1972.

When she arrived in Austin, there were no restroom facilities for women legislators. She had to use the female employees' restroom in the Capitol. It was only after Barbara Jordan was elected to the Senate and demanded a private restroom that one was provided for women legislators.

From the beginning, Farenthold saw women working in the Capitol who made far less money than their male counterparts. She also found that blacks and Mexican-Americans were not represented.

Farenthold was labeled "advocate of lost causes."

She called for tough controls on special interest groups, spoke out against an anti-riot bill because of its threat to civil rights, passed an antiquities bill which gave Texas its share of treasures and artifacts found in Texas waters and along the coast, and supported a bill that allowed district courts to pay up to twenty dollars a day to jurors with economic hardships. She was disappointed at her failure to pass legislation to establish a Governor's Committee on Children and Youth (Texas was the only state without one) or a state Human Relations Committee.

During her second term she became the leader of the reform coalition in the Texas House of Representatives. The group, nicknamed "The Dirty Dozen," was made up of African-Americans, Mexican-Americans, liberals, and a few Republicans. Farenthold set up a committee to investigate the Sharpstown scandal, a stock scandal. In that investigation Farenthold became known as the "den mother of the Dirty Thirty." She was also instrumental in the passage of the Texas Equal Legal Rights Amendment, a law for which women had been lobbying for twenty-five years.

## A Bid for Governor

Farenthold announced her candidacy for governor in 1972. She used women in key campaign positions. Her female supporters campaigned in supermarket parking lots, shopping malls, and small-town squares. Farenthold's campaign was understaffed and underfinanced. Her opponent was Dolph Briscoe, a wealthy Uvalde rancher and businessman. Briscoe got fifty-five percent of the vote to Farenthold's forty-five percent.

Her defeat did not stop her from continuing to work for the Democratic party. She became active on the national political scene. While she was campaigning for George McGovern for president at the Democratic National Convention in 1972, she became a possible candidate for vice-president on the Democratic ticket. Farenthold became the first woman in United States history nominated for vice-president and voted upon at the Democratic National Convention. She lost the place on the ticket to Thomas Eagleton, United States senator from Missouri. She continued campaigning for the Democrats as national co-chairperson of Citizens for McGovern. In 1973 she was elected chairwoman of the first National Women's Political Caucus in Houston.

On February 4, 1974, Farenthold again announced her candidacy for governor, challenging Briscoe. In her announcement speech she said: ". . . I went to a girl's preparatory school and a woman's college and never studied a thing about women's suffrage. I studied law but never studied one case about sex discrimination. The barriers are slowly being broken in Texas. At least now no one is strangling over a woman running for office."

Once again her campaign funds came mostly from women and Farenthold's family. People had forgotten the 1972 Sharpstown scandal and her push for reform in banking laws. They had forgotten the Equal Legal Rights Amendment which benefited women. Voters around the state were indifferent to the election and there was a low voter turnout. Briscoe won again, with Farenthold getting only twenty-eight percent of the votes.

## Academia

For the next two years she continued speaking on behalf of the National Women's Political Caucus. One of her engagements took her to Wells College in Aurora, New York. Academia was not unknown to Farenthold. She had served as an assistant professor of law at Texas Southern University and at the University of Houston. In 1976, when she was offered the job as president of Wells College, she accepted. She became the thirteenth and the first female president of the prestigious, all-girls college. She had the portraits of her all-male predecessors moved from her office to the library because "there wasn't a role model among them."

During her four-year tenure with the college she was instrumental in creating a network of programs aimed at helping women enter politics or run for political office, thereby creating role models for young women. She cleared a deficit in the budget, increased Wells' enrollment by recruiting nationwide, and brought national publicity to the college with her own speaking engagements.

In June 1978 Farenthold spoke to 3,000 people at a gay rally in Houston and called for an end to discrimination against the large minority. When asked why a "straight, white woman with four grown children is addressing this convocation of gay men and women," she replied, "The answer should be self-evident. No one is free unless we are all free."

## Back to Texas

Farenthold resigned from Wells College and returned

to Texas in May 1980. She and her family had traveled between New York and Texas for four years. She was ready to return to Houston to practice law. Texans began to speculate on what political role she would seek. She chose to speak only about women's issues and to encourage them to take an active role in state politics.

Farenthold believes that society needs to study history before there can be massive social change. She came to that conclusion from her own experiences and research. Two books dealing with race relations that had a great influence on her thinking were *Cry the Beloved Country* by Alan Patton and the *Autobiography of Malcolm X* by Malcolm X and Alex Haley. She spoke to both men and women when she said: "Ignorance reinforces tradition, ignorance reinforces stereotypes, ignorance reinforces privilege. That's why we need to know our history."

Frances Tarlton "Sissy" Farenthold has won a pioneer's place in the history of Texas politics by opening the doors of political activism to women. She urges women "to continue to open doors for each other, and to strive for a time when women will gain political support *not* in spite of being women, but because they are women."

# BETTE NESMITH GRAHAM
## 1924 - May 12, 1980

A TEXAS
FIRST
AS AN
INVENTOR
AND
BENEFACTOR

Bette Graham was a secretary and artist who used those skills to develop an office product that turned into a multi-million-dollar business. Today her Liquid Paper is used not only by secretaries, but by people all over the world. With the riches gained from her invention, she established two foundations devoted to helping women.

## A Young Artist

Bette Clair McMurray was born in San Antonio, Texas, in 1924. She was a shy girl and very sensitive to the things around her. During her school years she developed an eye for color and form. She also learned about the use of paints. She appreciated artists' works and decided to become an artist herself.

World War II started before Bette finished high school. Men all over the United States were called into duty. Young men quit their jobs or school to volunteer before they were drafted. There were many hasty marriages before the young men left for war. Following the trend, Bette quit school and married her childhood sweetheart. Her son Michael was born while his father was in military service. She was now a mother with a small child, waiting for her husband to come home.

*Bette Nesmith Graham (third from left).*

Many wartime marriages ended in divorce. Soldiers returned home after years to find their families had changed as much as they had. Women had become more independent and self-sufficient. They had substituted for men in higher paying factory and business jobs. After the war the women were expected to give those jobs back to men. Most people thought men needed to make more money than women because they were heads of households. They also thought it was only right that traditional male jobs go back to the men who had been away at war. Women were to go back to being housewives and mothers, or to low-paying jobs.

> ". . . women must learn to fight, but to fight with love.
> They must become more aggressive, and by that, I mean more confident of their abilities."
> —Bette Graham

## A Single Mother

Bette and her husband were marriage casualties of World War II. By the end of the war, Bette was a divorced mother with a child to support. Going back to school was impossible. She had to earn a living and had no marketable skills. Determined to provide for her son, she moved to Dallas to find work. She learned typing and shorthand and was hired as a secretary. Because she was a very hardworking and capable secretary, she was promoted to executive secretary for a bank president and earned $300 a month.

With her promotion and raise in salary, she was

given an electric typewriter. Graham had never used one before and found that it was very sensitive to the touch. She made more errors than when she used her manual typewriter and spent a lot of time correcting the mistakes. To make matters worse, the electric typewriter used carbon ribbons and smeared when an error was erased.

Graham did not want to waste time retyping letters, so she looked for a way to neatly cover her mistakes. As she thought about different possibilities, she thought about how she corrected mistakes when she painted. She often painted over a mistake on canvas. Why wouldn't the same principle work on paper?

**An Inventor**

"I decided to use what artists use," Graham said. "I put some tempera waterbase paint in a bottle and took my watercolor brush to the office, and I used that to correct my typing mistakes." Before Graham got to the point of taking her solution to work, she experimented in her kitchen. She began by mixing tempera paint with other chemicals in her electric mixer. She almost caught the kitchen on fire with one mixture on the stove. She ruined many saucepans and spent some sleepless nights before she came up with a workable mixture.

She did not tell anyone about her invention and her boss never noticed the corrections. It was not long before another secretary saw Graham correcting her mistakes with a brush. She asked Graham to give her some of the correcting fluid. Graham filled a small bottle and labeled it "Mistake Out." Soon other secretaries were asking for bottles of the correction fluid.

70

Graham wanted to improve her product, but she could not afford to pay someone to help her. She spent hours in the library researching tempera paint. A Dallas high school chemistry teacher helped her with formulas. By 1956 she was ready to start her own business, which she named Mistake Out Company. She later changed the name to Liquid Paper.

**A Businesswoman**

All of the supplies had to come out of her monthly salary. She worked nights to fill orders for her secretary friends. Graham decided to get a national company to market, advertise, and sell her product. She presented a proposal to International Business Machines (IBM). IBM was not interested. Graham made the decision to market Liquid Paper herself. She improved the formula, redesigned the bottles that held the liquid, and developed her own advertising campaign. She had to decide how much to charge for the product and how to get dealers to sell it.

All of the company's work had to be done after her regular job hours. She had to earn money to support herself and her son Michael, as well as buy supplies for her company. "It was hard to manage," Graham said, "but I felt, and still feel, that the best way for a company to grow is through its own productivity [and] efforts and not on a lot of borrowed money."

**Taking a Risk**

In 1958 Graham left her paid secretarial position to work full-time on marketing Liquid Paper. "The most difficult challenge was to overcome the fear of failure," she said. Graham entered into a man's world in starting her own business. There were few women active in the business world. She had no male to open business doors for her. She did not let that stop her.

Her kitchen became a laboratory to improve her product. Her garage was a manufacturing plant where Michael and his friends filled bottles at night. (Michael Nesmith was later a member of the rock group The Monkees.) After two years Graham was selling only one hundred bottles a month. At times she wanted to give up, but she did not. Instead she mailed articles about Liquid Paper to magazines read by office suppliers. Her break came in the October 1958 issue of *The Office*. The magazine listed Liquid Paper as one of its new products of the month.

Orders began coming in for small amounts. Then one day Graham received an order for more than four hundred bottles from General Electric, a large company. It was the first sign that her company could succeed. Secretaries from all over the United States began ordering Liquid Paper. Sales soon outgrew her kitchen, and she added a portable building in her backyard. She also hired a couple of college students to work part-time filling bottles. By 1962 she was selling up to three hundred bottles a week.

**A New Partner**

Bette married Robert Graham in 1962, and he joined her in expanding the company. By 1963 they were selling five hundred bottles a week. A year later they were bottling 5,000 bottles a week. The business outgrew the backyard portable building and her garage. Graham incorporated the company in 1965 and moved the business to a four-room house. By 1967 she had a million-dollar business.

The company eventually outgrew the four-room frame house and multiple portable buildings that had been added to the backyard. The Liquid Paper Corporation was then moved into a fully automated plant. Graham's nineteen employees no longer filled bottles by hand. They operated machinery that filled one million bottles the first year of operation. In ten years Graham had taken her company from selling one hundred bottles a month to 40,000 bottles a week.

Graham, a Christian Scientist, had always been a religious person. She maintained as high a standard in her business life as in her personal life. She treated her employees with respect and created a beautiful work environment for them. She helped design a building with park areas, fine arts, and a library. She valued the ideas and personal growth of her employees.

### Loss of Power

In 1968 Graham resigned as president of the corporation and became chairman of the board. In 1975 she and Robert Graham were divorced and she resigned from the board. Robert Graham took the top position in the company. Much to Bette Graham's dismay, the philosophy of the company changed. Also, the board decided to change the formula for Liquid Paper, which meant she would no longer get royalties from her invention. She later said that her resignation from the board "was a stupid thing to do, a stupid thing." Her husband had left her and she could no longer work with him. "But I would never have resigned if I had known that the philosophy of personal and corporate growth on which I founded the company would not be carried out," she explained.

In 1976 Graham became a Christian Scientist practitioner and devoted more of her time to her religion. She also set up the Bette Clair McMurray Foundation, which was to be financed by her royalties from Liquid Paper. Graham owned nearly half of the stock in the Liquid Paper Corporation. When Gillette Company paid $47.8 million for the corporation in 1979, Graham negotiated the sale of her invention and recovered her royalty rights. The sale reinstated her royalty contract, which furnished funds for the Bette Claire McMurray Foundation to continue its work.

The primary purpose of the foundation was to help women find new ways to earn a living. Over the years it financed a career guidance program for unwed mothers, career counseling and shelters for battered women, and college scholarships for older women to help upgrade their jobs. In 1978 Graham set up the Gihon Foundation to help women reach their full potential.

Graham succeeded in business when it was a man's world and left a legacy of hope for potential businesswomen. Through her generosity and leadership in establishing two foundations, many women have better lives. Before her death on May 12, 1980, Graham said, "Most people in my income bracket build estates. I can't understand why. My estate will be what I do for others."

Bette Nesmith Graham learned "to fight with love." She not only left a fortune in money, she left a very rich estate in what she did for women.

# OVETA CULP HOBBY
## January 19, 1905 - August 16, 1995

A TEXAS
FIRST IN
THE
WOMEN'S
ARMY
CORPS

At the age of twenty, Oveta Culp Hobby was appointed the first woman parliamentarian in the Texas House of Representatives. She was the first commanding officer of the Women's Army Auxiliary Corps (WAAC), the first woman awarded the Distinguished Service Medal, and the first secretary of the Department of Health, Education, and Welfare (HEW). Hobby devoted her life to the service of the community and country.

### Cherokee Name

Oveta Culp was born on January 19, 1905, in Killeen, Texas. She was the second child in a family of seven children born to Ike W. and Emma Elizabeth (Hoover) Culp. Her mother named her Oveta after a character in a romance novel. The Cherokee word means "forget." The name also rhymed with Juanita, Oveta's older sister. Oveta once complained that her name had been misspelled and mispronounced all of her life.

Ike W. Culp was a lawyer and a politician. He served as a state legislator and encouraged Oveta's interest in law and politics. She sometimes visited him in Austin when the legislature was in session. When he was in Killeen, she stopped by his office after school to see if there

*Oveta Culp Hobby*

—Courtesy William P. Hobby

was something she could do to help him. By the time she was ten years old she was reading the *Congressional Record*. She later said, "My father expected a lot of me. He was the one who always kept after me to do my best. Certainly my mother and father didn't categorize what was for a girl and what was for a boy to do."

*"My father taught me I could turn the world around just as well as my brothers."*
—Oveta Culp Hobby

Emma Hoover Culp took care of her seven children and her widowed mother's business affairs. She was a dedicated suffragist and was active in politics. She left her older daughters home to can fruits from the orchard while she campaigned for William Pettus Hobby in his race for governor. She endorsed Hobby's election because he had gotten the bill through the legislature so women could vote that year. Oveta remembered her mother saying as she went out the back door, "Girls, you will have to look out for the peaches, I'm going out to campaign for Will Hobby." Mrs. Culp also believed in service to the less fortunate in the community. She collected food, clothing, and money for the poor. Oveta often delivered baskets of goods to neighbors who were going through hard times.

**A Mind of Her Own**

Oveta was influenced by her parents, but she always had a mind of her own. She was about six years old when a temperance campaign reached its peak in Killeen. At Sunday school all the small children were asked to wear a white ribbon from the Woman's Christian Temperance Union and to sign a pledge that they would never drink liquor. Oveta refused to sign the pledge. She did not intend to drink liquor but she did not want to give her pledge unless she intended to keep it forever.

Oveta attended public schools in Killeen and played with neighborhood friends as well as her siblings. One of their games was playing chase. They were chased by cowboys and Indians. She liked the drama of the game because she thought she wanted to be an actress.

Oveta was an avid reader as a child. She had to be pulled away from her books for family outings. By the time she was in sixth grade, she was the best speller in the school. When the teacher announced that a Bible would be the prize in a spelling contest, Oveta told her that "she might as well write [Oveta's] name in the Bible there and then."[4] She won the Bible. In later years when she was asked if she played bridge, she replied that she did not and said, "I'll bet I've read 2,000 books in my life that I wouldn't have read if I had played bridge."

## A Legislative Observer

When Ike Culp was elected to the state legislature in 1919, he took fourteen-year-old Oveta to Austin with him. She observed each day's session and became interested in the issues debated by House members. She missed almost a semester of school but still graduated from Temple High School in the high group of her class.

During her high school years she took elocution

(public speaking) to satisfy her interest in drama. She recited "Alaska, the Brave Cowgirl" so dramatically that she was offered a theater touring contract. Her parents refused to allow her to accept the offer, so she organized her own group. The "Jolly Entertainers," a group of teenage musicians, toured neighboring towns and gave benefit performances to raise money to buy church organs.

After high school Oveta studied at Mary Hardin Baylor College in Belton, taught elocution, and put on school plays. When her father was elected to a second term in the Texas House of Representatives, she moved to Austin and became a cub reporter on the *Austin Statesman.* She began auditing law courses at the University of Texas law school. By the time she was nineteen, she had an extensive library of 750 volumes. Her collection included *Cases of Common Law Reading, Revised Civil Statutes, Jefferson and Hamilton,* and the poetry of Edna St. Vincent Millay. Oveta said that her father always complained about "my sister's clothing bills and my book bills."

## A Young Legislative Parliamentarian

In 1925 twenty-year-old Oveta was appointed as legislative parliamentarian by the Speaker of the Texas House of Representatives. She continued her education with tutors and classes at the University of Texas law school. She became a legal clerk of the State Banking Commission. By 1928 Oveta had codified the banking laws. She served as parliamentarian again in 1939 and 1941. She later wrote a book on parliamentary procedure based on her experiences in the legislature.

Oveta was active in local organizations of the Democratic party. She went to Houston in 1928 to help with the National Democratic Convention. She then worked on a Houston mayoral campaign. Her candidate won and offered her a job as assistant to the city attorney. At the age of twenty-five she was persuaded to run for the state legislature. Her opponent, backed by the Ku Klux Klan, defeated her. She never again entered elective politics.

**Marriage and a New Career**

Former governor William Pettus Hobby was president of the *Post-Dispatch* newspaper in Houston. Oveta's mother had campaigned for him when he ran for governor and Mr. Culp was a close friend. Oveta and Hobby began attending the symphony and social engagements together. They were married on February 23, 1931; she was twenty-six and he was fifty-three. She said that when Hobby arrived for their wedding, her father told him, "Will, she'll embarrass you. She doesn't give a hang about clothes." She had always been too interested in books, politics, and horseback riding to pay attention to how she dressed.

After their marriage, Oveta Culp Hobby joined her husband at the *Post-Dispatch*. She worked as researcher, book editor, assistant editor, and executive vice-president. The first of their two children, William Pettus, Jr., was born on Mrs. Hobby's birthday, January 19, 1932. Five years later, on January 19, 1937, again on Oveta's birthday, Jessica Oveta was born. It was during her pregnancy with Jessica that Mrs. Hobby wrote *Mr. Chairman,* which was adopted as a textbook by the Texas public schools in 1938. The Hobbys bought an almost bankrupt *Houston Post* in 1939. They worked as a team to pay off its large debt.

In 1941 the United States had begun its first peacetime draft for men. Women wrote the War Department to learn how they could serve their country. Mrs. Hobby was asked to organize a section on women's activities for the army. She turned down the offer but agreed to draw up an organizational chart with recommendations on ways women could serve. Gen. David Searles asked her to come to Washington to put the plan in operation. She refused, but her husband told her, "You must do whatever your country asks you to do."

## World War II and the WAC

Oveta Hobby became head of the Women's Interest Section of the War Department Bureau of Public Relations. She studied the French and British women's armies and proposed a plan for the United States to avoid their mistakes. She was on her way to Houston from Washington when Pearl Harbor was attacked on December 7, 1941. She called her husband and they both agreed that she must return to Washington. President Franklin D. Roosevelt had declared World War II by the time she arrived. She went to work immediately to identify jobs that women could do with the least special training. Then she presented her plan for a women's army to Congress. When she was asked for a list of women who could command a women's army, she left her name off the list. Gen. George C. Marshall asked Hobby to accept the command.

Her husband agreed with Marshall. "It would never have crossed my mind to command an army of women. I never did learn to salute properly or master the 30-inch stride," she later said.

When the Women's Army Auxiliary Corps (WAAC) was created in May 1942, Hobby was its director. The WAACs did not have full army standing, which created problems in requests for uniforms and barracks. Hobby had one uniform which she washed and ironed each night. She wore a flattering hard-brimmed hat that became known as the "Hobby Hat." In 1943 "Auxiliary" was dropped from the groups name when the Women's Army Corps (WAC) received full army status. Hobby became a colonel and fought for equal treatment for her "G.I. Janes." The job list for women increased from fifty-four to 239 during the war. Women served as riveters, interpreters, balloon-gas chemists, surveyors, and boiler inspectors. She later remarked that women working during the war "had a tremendous influence in moving women into the labor force—not only those who served in the military, but also those who held jobs in factories and other war-related jobs."

Exhausted from years of long days and nights as commander of the WACs, Hobby resigned her command in 1945. Later she was the first woman to receive the Distinguished Service Medal. She returned to Houston to continue her career as director of the Hobby-owned KPCR radio and KPCR-TV, and as executive vice-president of the *Houston Post*.

**Another Washington Assignment**

When Dwight D. Eisenhower became president of the United States in 1952, he appointed Hobby as chairperson of the Federal Security Act (FSA). On April 11, 1953, she became the first secretary of the new Department of Health, Education, and Welfare (HEW). She once again had to organize a new branch of the federal government.

During her tenure at HEW, she introduced many changes. The Salk vaccine for polio was released and made available for both children and adults, and benefits were extended for the self-employed. On the lighter side, she was chosen as one of the best-dressed women in America, much to her daughter's embarrassment. She was also pronounced "the best man in the Cabinet." As the second woman Cabinet member in the nation's history, her dress, words, and actions often made newspaper headlines.

When her husband became ill in 1955, Hobby resigned her job and returned to Houston. She had balanced her life between family and government responsibilities for years. She was ready to be home with her family. She became president and editor of the *Houston Post* and oversaw their communications business. Although she was often asked to return to public life, she would not leave her husband's side. William Pettus Hobby died in Houston on June 3, 1964. William P. Hobby, Jr., joined his mother at the *Post* until he was elected lieutenant governor of Texas in 1972. She continued to run the Hobby empire. She also served on numerous university and college boards and on local, state, and national committees until poor health dictated her retirement.

Hobby received many awards and honors for her lifetime of work for the United States government, the state of Texas, and the Houston community. Thirty years after she received the Distinguished Service Medal, she was awarded the Marshall Medal for Public Service, the highest award given by the Association of the United States Army. She was the first woman to receive the two awards. In 1984 she was named to the Texas Women's Hall of Fame.

Hobby once said, "The woman who has reached a top position in management usually has a much more difficult time in winning acceptance than a man in a comparable position." When she was questioned about the key to her own success, she said, "Oh, it's the easiest thing in the world. All you have to do is be equal. And don't go into whatever you're doing with a chip on your shoulder."

Oveta Culp Hobby was equal to the task at hand until her death on August 16, 1995.

# MARY AUSTIN HOLLEY
## October 30, 1784 - August 2, 1846

Mary Austin Holley was the first woman to write about the lives and times of early Texas. After her first visit to Texas in 1831, Holley wrote *Texas Observations, Historical, Geographical, and Descriptive, in a Series of Letters Written During a Visit to Austin's Colony, with a View to a Permanent Settlement in That Country in the Autumn of 1831.* In spite of the long and awkward title, the book was an immediate success. It had a great influence on the growth of colonization in Texas.

**Childhood**

Mary Austin was born on October 30, 1784, in New Haven, Connecticut. Her father, Elijah Austin, was a merchant who sent ships to China to purchase tea, spices, carpets, and silks to sell in his store. He often took Mary and her three older brothers to the wharf with him to see the ships come in and watch the men unload the cargo. Mary thought her father lived a very exciting life.

Ester Phelps Austin, Mary's mother, had no interest in business or politics. She devoted her time to caring for her eight children and entertaining the families many relatives who lived in or around New Haven. Mrs. Austin

*Mary Austin Holley*
—Courtesy Institute of Texan Cultures,
UT San Antonio

86

grew up in a wealthy family where the children were sent to the best schools available. She taught her own children to respect education.

Mary was a fast learner as well as a natural musician. She learned to write neatly and spell correctly. Along with her book studies, she learned sewing, knitting, embroidery, and drawing. Math was not considered important for females, so she had very little instruction in numbers.

> *"This theme of Texas united [Holley's] deepest interests— romantic love of nature and the vision of a new nation rising under the aegis [sponsorship] of the Austins."*

### A Shipwreck

The comfortable life of the Austins ended in 1794, when Elijah Austin died of yellow fever. In the months before his death, Austin had organized a company to build a much larger ship for the Chinese trade. He had invested everything he had and all he could borrow to build the forty-eight-thousand-dollar vessel. Soon after Austin's death, the new ship wrecked at sea and was lost. The family home and most of its furnishings had to be sold to try to pay investors. Mrs. Austin was left with only one-third of the real estate owned by her husband. The children were left nothing.

Mary was old enough to understand that their lives were changing forever. Her brothers forgot about college and looked for jobs. Timothy Phelps, Esther Austin's brother, asked Mary to live with him and his new wife. Mary attended a female academy where she learned to write and speak French. She was included at dinners when the Phelpses entertained prominent guests. It was from the lively discussions at the dinners and from her own reading that she learned the most. She also learned how to design and make her own clothes.

One of the advantages of living in New Haven was the opportunity for girls to meet young men from Yale. Horace Holley enrolled at Yale in 1799. He was handsome and an excellent speaker. Fifteen-year-old Mary was impressed by his voice and appearance. She was attending a new Union School, established by Noah Webster. She was a good student and loved the classroom and the library. She had already decided she wanted more from life than being just a housewife.

**Marriage**

Mary was not a striking beauty, but she impressed people with her maturity, ladylike conduct, and stylish dress. She played the guitar and piano and sang. Horace Holley came to appreciate Mary's wit and intelligence. After he graduated from Yale and went to New York to study law, they exchanged spirited letters about their interests. When he gave up the study of law and returned to New Haven to attend the seminary to study theology, he began to court Mary seriously. Mary Austin and Horace Holley were married on January 1, 1805.

The newly ordained Reverend Holley accepted his first ministry at Greenfield Hill, a small community near New Haven, in the fall of 1805. The Holleys were happy in Greenfield Hill but realized they would have to make more money if they were going to have a family. In December 1808, the month their daughter Harriette was born, Horace accepted an appointment at South End Church in Boston.

They rented a large house where they could once again entertain. After three years of managing the large household and constantly entertaining, Mary's health began to deteriorate. In 1811 they rented an apartment and their meals were prepared and served from their landlord's kitchen. The arrangement freed Mary to enjoy her music again, take daily walks, read at leisure, and travel out of town. It was during that time that she began to keep a journal of her travels.

**Recognized Writer**

In 1818 Horace Holley was elected president of Transylvania University in Lexington, Kentucky. While he was there making arrangements for the family to move, Mary gave birth to their son on July 19, and named him Horace after his father. The Holleys became leaders in the social and academic life of Lexington. While Mary became known as a writer, President Holley dealt with problems at the university. But those were put aside in Mary's mind when Harriette became engaged to William Brand, son of a wealthy businessman. Harriette and William were married in 1825.

President Holley tried to smooth over the religious misunderstandings between him and the trustees, but he failed. In 1827 he resigned from Transylvania University and planned to begin a college in New Orleans. He received some financial help in New Orleans, but he was disappointed at the enrollment and closed the school after a month. Holley then decided to take his family east until time for the fall semester, when he planned to return and begin again.

Both of the Holleys became ill with yellow fever on the voyage to New York. Mr. Holley died on ship on July 31, 1827. Mary was so sick that she was only vaguely aware of the sound of pistols and splash of water when he was buried at sea.

Mary returned to Boston. She decided to write a memoir about her husband's achievements in the ministry and in education. She left nine-year-old Horace in Cambridge under the care of a Mr. Wells for his education. Her son had emotional and mental problems that made him, in his mother's words, "a child of misfortune ever." Harriette was expecting her second child and begged her mother to come to Lexington to stay with them.

## A Widow's Tribute

In Lexington, Mary began asking the Holley family and friends to send letters and anecdotes about her deceased husband. Dr. Charles Caldwell brought her a speech he had made about Holley's achievements and offered it for her use. In 1828 the memoir was published under the name *Caldwell's Discourse*. Although Mary's name was not on the book, she was recognized as the writer.

With her project finished, Holley had to make some decisions. She was forty-five years old and had no means of support. Her daughter wanted her to stay in Lexington. Holley did not like domesticity when she was young, and she did not want to settle into a rocking chair holding grandbabies.

When she went to New Orleans to settle her husband's affairs, she met the Labranches, a wealthy French family. She became governess to Melazie Labranche and was allowed to bring her son Horace to the Good Hope Plantation, owned by the Labranches. They often stayed in their town house in New Orleans, where Holley heard enthusiastic talk about the land available in Stephen F. Austin's colony in the Mexican state of Texas.

**Texas Calls**

Holley began corresponding with her cousin, Stephen F. Austin. He set aside a league of land for her in his colony. Holley's favorite brother, Henry, lived in Texas and encouraged her to visit him. In October 1831 she left New Orleans and traveled by ship to the mouth of the Brazos River, where Henry met her and took her to his log house in Bolivar.

She realized how useful a travel book would be for the immigrants coming to Texas. She kept a detailed journal and stacks of notebooks describing the countryside. Stephen F. Austin visited her and talked about his plans for the colony and the problems with Mexico.

Holley's first book, *Texas . . . ,* published in 1833, was a success. When she returned to Texas for a short visit in the spring of 1835, Texas had changed. The settlers were talking about war with Mexico. Stephen F. Austin was in prison in Mexico City. Holley spent her short time there sketching and outlining another book on Texas.

By the time her second book, *Mrs. Holley's Texas,* was printed in July 1836, Texas was a free republic. She lobbied for the United States to recognize the Republic of Texas as an independent country. Even after Stephen F. Austin's death, Texas called to her. She returned to her land grant on Galveston Island, but she soon ran out of money. Holley then returned to New Orleans to teach the children of her first pupil, Melazie Labranche.

Mary Austin Holley, a Texan at heart, died of yellow fever in New Orleans on August 2, 1846. She expressed her own legacy to Texas when she wrote: "I little anticipated . . . I should one day become the historian of a Nation, or the biographer of [Stephen F. Austin] who brought it into being. I am an Austin."

# ELIZABETH E. "LIZZIE" JOHNSON
## 1843 - October 9, 1924

| A TEXAS FIRST IN THE RANCHING BUSINESS |
|---|

Elizabeth E. "Lizzie" Johnson was the first, and probably only, Texas woman who owned her own cattle and ran them under her own brand up the Chisholm Trail. She had her husband sign a pre-nuptial agreement long before it was even considered an acceptable thing to do. She was a shrewd businesswoman and a pioneer among women in the field of finance.

**Childhood**

Lizzie Johnson was a juvenile miser. As a child she saved as much money as she could. She even saved her own hair ribbons and borrowed others from someone else to wear.

She was born in Jefferson City, Missouri, in 1843, the second of six children born to Professor Thomas Jefferson and Catherine Hyde Johnson. Professor Johnson moved to the Republic of Texas as a Presbyterian missionary and teacher in the late 1840s. He established the Johnson Institute in Hays County in 1852. The institute was the first school of higher learning west of the Colorado River in Texas.

When Professor Johnson was looking for property to build his school, he was offered the land which is now

*Elizabeth E. "Lizzie" Johnson*
—Courtesy Institute of Texan Cultures,
UT San Antonio

the University of Texas in Austin. He refused the offer because of his opposition to liquor and drinking. A very religious man, Johnson wanted to protect his students from city life. He chose a rural setting about seventeen miles from Austin. His beliefs about alcohol and religion influenced Lizzie all of her life.

The Johnson Institute was originally planned as a boys' school. However, so many applications were made by girls that the institute became coeducational. Many of the students attended the school from the first grade through what would today be considered a college degree. The institute charged twelve dollars a month for board, tuition and washing for students under fourteen years old, and fifteen dollars per month for those older than fourteen. The curriculum stressed spelling and grammar and was known for teaching the highest mathematics known at that time. Lizzie and her siblings attended the institute, but Lizzie received a diploma from Chapel Hill, Texas.

*". . . the trip [Chisholm Trail] was . . . an adventure that tested the courage and endurance of sturdy men, and was considered entirely too dangerous to be undertaken by a woman."*

## Teacher

Lizzie began teaching when she was sixteen. She was considered "austere and firm" by her students. She taught French, arithmetic, bookkeeping, and spelling. The institute had the first piano in Hays County, which Lizzie used to teach music in addition to her other duties.

She taught at her father's school for several years, but left to teach in Manor, Lockhart, and Austin because she could make more money there. She added to her teacher's income by writing magazine and newspaper articles, as well as selling stories to the *Frank Leslie Magazine*. Lizzie was very secretive about her writing and how much money she made. She was also paid to keep books for area cattlemen.

The money she made was not hoarded. Lizzie began investing in stocks. She bought $2,500 worth of stock in the Evans, Snider, Bewell Cattle Company of Chicago. After three years she sold the stock for almost ten times what she had paid for it. She also invested in real estate and bought a large two-story house on Second Street in Austin to open a private school. She lived on the second floor and conducted the school on the first floor.

## Civil War

During the Civil War (1861-1865), most of the Texas men and boys were in the army. Women and children were left to take care of farms and cattle. They could not do all of the work required to run a ranch. There were no fences and the cattle strayed from one area to another. Unclaimed herds roamed the plains and countryside. Newborn calves were not branded and their number increased each year.

The Union controlled the Mississippi River and cut off the Texas beef supply. There was no market for Texas cattle. Thousands of the animals were killed for hide and tallow while meat was left to rot or be eaten by buzzards. While the "skinning war" was taking place in Texas, the supply of beef was scarce in the North. Texas cattlemen began looking toward the North to market their stock.

While most young women were trying to attract eligible young men, Johnson was more interested in starting her own herd of cattle. During the week she taught school, but on weekends she drove her buggy through the brush to round up unbranded longhorns. Even though she realized there was more money in the cattle business than in teaching children, she did not give up her school. By the age of twenty-eight, she had put together a respectable herd of cattle. On June 1, 1871, Elizabeth Johnson registered her mark and brand in the Travis County Record Book.

**Marriage**

Johnson was thirty-six years old when she married Hezekiah G. Williams on June 8, 1879. Williams, a preacher, was a handsome widower with six children. Although it was scandalous at the time, Johnson insisted on Williams signing a prenuptial agreement. Everything she owned or any profits she made would remain solely hers, and in her business she used her maiden name, Elizabeth Johnson. The couple lived in Johnson's apartment above her private school, and she continued to teach, write stories, and invest in cattle.

Williams was not as good in business matters as Johnson, but he went into the cattle business too. Two years after their marriage, he registered his own mark and brand. Johnson and Williams used different brands because they kept all business separate and independent of each other. Johnson frequently loaned her husband money to get him out of bad business deals. She had him sign a note and insisted he repay the loan on time.

When Johnson and Williams picked out cattle to buy, she made the best choice for herself. She said Williams "would keep his too long before selling and lose money anyway." They used the same ranch foreman and had him steal unbranded cattle from each other. Johnson's brother Will often joked that "while Hezekiah was preaching on Sunday, his sons were out stealing his congregation's cattle."

### Chisholm Trail

Williams was a drinking man and Johnson did not trust him to take both of their herds to market. It was unheard of for a woman to make a trail drive where she would be alone with a group of men for months at a time. That did not stop Johnson. She was going to take her own herd up the Chisholm Trail. She and Williams rode in a buckboard behind the two herds. Johnson insisted their herds be kept separate on the drive. Her cowhands were also ordered to steal Williams' unbranded cattle and brand them as her own.

Johnson dressed in calicoes and cottons with yards of gathered skirt over several petticoats. She wore a gray bonnet and shawl, and gloves to protect her soft, pretty hands. She was a combination of cattleman and southern lady. The cowboys treated her like a lady and put a rope around her wagon to keep the snakes out at night. Johnson made the trip several times before the trail closed in 1889.

**Businesswoman**

The cattle boom ended when farmers began putting up fences to protect their farms. They were tired of trail drives that tore down their fences and ruined their crops. A fight began between the farmers and cattlemen. States passed laws upholding the farmers' rights, so that cattle drives could not follow the Chisholm Trail. There was no longer a large profit to be made on Texas cattle.

When the Chisholm Trail closed, Johnson gave up teaching. She was keeping books for large cattle companies and still writing. She had made a small fortune on cattle and no longer needed the money from her school. Johnson began buying city lots and buildings in Austin. She owned real estate in Llano, Hays, and Trinity counties, and small ranches in Culbertson and Jeff Davis counties. She was very secretive about her business and made decisions without the advice of others or the knowledge of her husband.

Johnson and Williams owned one ranch together. The Williams Ranch had several thousand acres and was located near Driftwood in Hays and Blanco counties. Hays City was established on the ranch. It had two streets—one named Williams and the other named Johnson. They built a church and tried, unsuccessfully, to move the county seat from San Marcos to Hays City.

After Johnson gave up her school, the couple did not spend much time in Austin or on their ranch. They spent the winters in St. Louis at luxurious hotels. Johnson had spurts of self-indulgence and bought dresses made of silk, taffeta, and velvet. Her dresses and coats were lined with expensive materials and were made to show off her eighteen-inch waist. On trips to New York, she bought thousands of dollars worth of diamond rings, earrings, pins, necklaces, and hair ornaments. She dressed to impress people around her in her travels.

One of their trips took them to Cuba, where they lived for several years. There was a good market for their cattle there. According to a family legend, Williams was kidnapped by bandits while they were in Cuba. He was held for $50,000 ransom. Johnson paid the ransom in cash and he was returned safely to her. She brought Williams back to Texas along with a talking parrot, her companion for many years.

Johnson felt no need to impress people in Austin. She wore simpler, plainer clothes and even changed her hairstyle to a severe knot on the top of her head. Many of her extravagant clothes and jewels were packed away. Some were never worn again.

### Williams' Death

Williams was in poor health for the last twenty-five years of his life. While he could still travel, Johnson took him to Hot Springs, Arkansas, and other health spas in the United States to try to improve his health. Mrs. John E. Shelton, Johnson's niece, recalled that "when he got real sick, [Johnson] wagged him off to his sons to take care of." Johnson had never liked her husband's children by his first marriage.

Hezekiah Williams died in El Paso, Texas, in 1914.

They had been married thirty-five years. Johnson brought his body back to Austin to be buried. When she paid six hundred dollars for his coffin, she wrote across the undertaker's bill, "I loved this old buzzard this much."

Johnson was deeply saddened by her husband's death. She continued her business dealings but did not seem to care how she looked. She confided in and trusted no one and lived alone on her ranch. But her tongue was just as sharp as ever. Occasionally on a trip to town she would see Maj. George W. Littlefield, a bank owner and an active cattleman. She always yelled across the street, "Hello, you old cattle thief!"

## Declining Years

During the last few years of her life, Johnson lived in one room in the Brueggerhoff Building, which she owned in Austin. In spite of her wealth, she allowed herself no luxuries and few necessities. Each day she went to the post office dressed in a ragged black skirt, a dirty bonnet or hood, and the old gray shawl she had worn for over forty years. Several times people offered her a dime thinking she was poor and hungry. She took the money. Not one to spend money needlessly, Johnson even bargained for her lunch. Mrs. Shelton said, "She sure didn't like prices going up—especially when she was on the paying end. When she moved up to that room she told the restaurant owner down on the ground floor that she wanted a bowl of soup every day for lunch as long as she lived and she paid him five years in advance to seal the bargain." The soup was ten cents a bowl.

Johnson was as miserly with others as she was with

herself. She heated the Brueggerhoff Building with wood she kept locked in one room. She gave the tenants one stick at a time. She insured that people were nice to her by pretending to consider donations to churches, schools, and even the University of Texas, but she had no intention of giving away her money. Johnson saw her relatives only when she wanted something from them. But in spite of her contrariness, a niece and nephew looked after her. Mrs. Shelton took Johnson into her home rather than allow her to become a ward of the county for the last year of her life.

Elizabeth "Lizzie" Johnson Williams died on October 9, 1924, without leaving a will. She was buried next to Hezekiah Williams at Oakwood Cemetery in Austin. Her heirs inherited more than a quarter of a million dollars in cash, jewelry, cattle, and real estate.

The things found hidden in the Brueggerhoff Building after Johnson's death added to the legends and romance surrounding her life: hundreds of dollars in five-dollar bills; thousands of dollars in one-hundred-dollar bills; jewels wrapped in a scorched cloth; parrot feathers and dried flowers from her husband's funeral wreaths; fancy dresses that had never been worn.

A colorful character until her death, Lizzie Johnson opened the door for Texas women in the cattle trade and in the field of finance. She earned the title of "Cattle Queen of Texas."

# MARGARET VIRGINIA "MARGO" JONES
## December 12, 1911 - July 24, 1955

Margaret "Margo" Virginia Jones was the first female director and producer of a professional theater. She won many awards for her achievements and was the only woman named as an outstanding director of little-theater outside New York City. She established the first professional theater-in-the-round in the United States and wrote a reference book on the technique. Her dream was to see a good theater in every town across the United States.

**Always a Director**

Margaret Virginia Jones, nicknamed "Margo," liked to dress in grownup clothes and imagine herself in another world of make-believe. Whether it was at play or putting on plays for others in Livingston, Texas, Jones liked to tell others what to do.

Her parents, Richard and Martha Pearl Jones, encouraged their children to be independent and creative. Her mother taught foreign languages, art, and music in the local schools to support the family while her father studied law at the University of Texas in Austin. There were four Jones children: Stella Nell (1909),

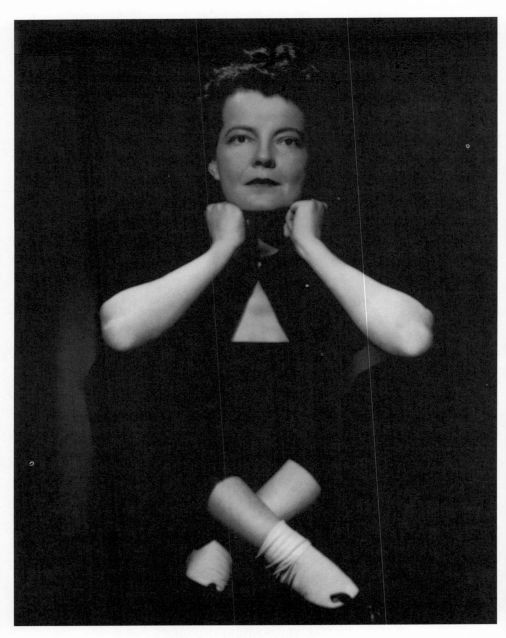

*Margaret Virginia "Margo" Jones*
—Courtesy Dallas Public Library

Margo (1911), Richard (1915), and Charles (1920). They were Jones' first theater company.

By the time she was eleven, Jones had her sister and brothers acting in plays for her parents and neighbors. She didn't act in the plays. She wrote and directed them. She told everyone else what to do and what to say. She created the sets and sold tickets to the productions. Even though she wrote and directed plays, Jones did not dream of becoming a director of experimental drama. Until she was eleven years old, she planned to become a lawyer like her father. She loved going to the courtroom with him when he presented a case before a judge and jury. She saw it as a great, suspenseful drama.

*"I was lucky to know so early what I wanted to do.*
*It gave me a valuable head start."*
— Margo Jones

## A Tragic Loss

When Jones was thirteen, a greater drama affected her life. There was an influenza epidemic in Livingston. Jones and her sister, Stella Nell, both caught the flu. In late December 1924, a winter storm hit Livingston, leaving a sheen of icicles hanging from the trees and houses. After weeks of being confined to their parents' bedroom, Jones begged her fifteen-year-old sister to slip outside and bring her an icicle. Stella Nell went out on the balcony in the ice and cold and got the icicle for her. Stella Nell began to cough and her nose started to bleed. She died ten days later. "I didn't think I could go on," Jones later said.

She decided that she must achieve greatness not only for herself, but for Stella Nell. By the time she was fourteen, she knew that she was not interested in practicing law. After she saw her first professional play, *Cyrano de Bergerac,* in Fort Worth, she knew what she wanted to do.

Jones had already skipped one grade in school before Stella Nell's death. After her death, Jones doubled her course load and, at the age of fifteen, graduated with Stella Nell's class. Although she was younger than her senior classmates, she was popular with the students. She won prizes for debate, speeches, and humorous readings. When Jones seemed to become serious about one young man who was a few years older than she, her parents encouraged her to go away to school.

## A Drama Student

Jones enrolled as a drama student at Texas State College for Women (now Texas Woman's University) at Denton. The college did not have a drama department, so she majored in speech and minored in education. All of the girls in her classes wanted to act. Women were expected to act or work on costumes, but Margo had no interest in acting. She wanted to direct.

Margo Jones was not willing to give up her dream just because it was not considered a field for women. She began to learn everything she could about stage production. A teacher suggested that Jones read plays to learn about what made a good script. Jones decided to read a

106

play a day. The habit of reading a script a day stayed with her for the rest of her life.

Jones garnered many important things from her reading. She saw how good plays were developed, and she learned how to keep the audience interested in the characters, and how actors expressed anger, fear, joy. She even studied psychology so she could better understand human emotions and actions. She also learned the importance of set design, costumes, and lighting.

She was nineteen years old in 1933 when she finished her master's degree. It was in the middle of the Great Depression, and many people were out of work. The day after she graduated Jones went to Southwestern School of Theater in Dallas and asked for a scholarship. She arrived at the theater in the midst of chaos. Everyone was trying to get a show ready to open. Jones jumped in to help and got the scholarship.

## An Internship

For several months she took classes and learned about method acting, sets, makeup, playwriting, dance, and music. She never acted in a play, but she was always in the background helping and learning about experimental theater. In the summer of 1934, she enrolled at the Pasadena Playhouse Summer School in California. Jones was the only woman interested in directing. She was chosen to stage manage the group's first production and co-direct the final summer play.

When the summer session ended, Jones got her first directing job at a community theater in Ojai, California. She lived with Shila Wardall, a wealthy young widow who was interested in acting. In 1935 Wardall asked Jones to go around the world with her. Wardall offered to pay all of her expenses plus a small salary for Jones to help edit a book that Wardall's deceased husband had written. Jones saw it as an opportunity to go to theaters in Japan, China, India, England, and France. She accepted the offer. After touring around the world, the ship docked in New York. "My first glimpse of New York," she said, "was the greatest thrill of all."

America was still in the grip of the Great Depression. Jones heard about a government program called the Federal Theater for unemployed writers, directors, and actors. She applied for and became the assistant director at the Houston Federal Theater, sponsored by the Houston Recreation Department. Unfortunately, the program lasted only a few months.


**Theater-in-the-Round**

Jones believed that the theater could mean and do much for the culture of a country. She attended the Moscow Art Theatre Festival and returned to Houston full of idealism and enthusiasm. She had one great ambition: to create the most exciting theater in America. "I saw no reason," she said, "why I couldn't have it in Houston."

Jones went to work with the Recreation Department of Houston in the fall of 1936. She discovered that the department owned an unused, vacant building. She persuaded the department to let her use the building free of charge to produce plays. Jones established the Houston Community Players. The building was not air conditioned and could not be used during the summer. Jones convinced the Lamar Hotel to allow her to use its air conditioned Grand Ballroom and produced the first theater-in-the-round outside of New York City. The audience sat in chairs surrounding the performers in the center. They had never attended theater where the spectators were so close to the actors. They loved it. When she was asked if she invented theater-in-the-round, she replied, "No, honey, the Greeks did."

Jones, the first director and producer to establish a highly acclaimed professional theater company in Texas, was named the Director of the South in 1939. She was also named one of twelve outstanding directors of little-theater outside New York City. Jones was the only woman selected in that group of twelve.

## Professional Theater in Texas

In the 1940s, Jones' motto became, "Put up or shut up!" With a $10,000 contribution, Jones set up a board of directors and officially incorporated as Dallas Theater, Inc. in 1947. She produced plays by Tennessee Williams and William Inge which were later produced on Broadway. Jones was recognized nationwide as having established the first professional theater-in-the-round in the United States. In 1951 she wrote *Theatre-in-the-Round,* which is still used as a reference book in producing and directing arena plays.

Jones spent her career trying to decentralize American theater. She believed that more actors, writers, directors, producers, and technicians could contribute to the theater world if there were resident theaters across America. In 1950 Jones wrote, "I . . . like to think that if I decided to take a cross-country trip along in 1960 I could stop in every city with a population of seventy-five thousand and see a good play well done."

Margo Jones did not live to see the results of her work or the influence she made on American theater in her short forty-four years. She died on July 24, 1955, after she was exposed to an odorless cleaning fluid that was used in her apartment at the Stoneleigh Hotel in Dallas. Even in death, she is still a living legend in the theater world.

# LUCY ANN THORNTON KIDD-KEY
## November 15, 1839–September 13, 1916

| A TEXAS FIRST AS A COLLEGE PRESIDENT |
|---|

Lucy Ann Thornton Kidd-Key was the first woman president of a college in Texas. In her twenty-eight years as president of North Texas Female College, she built an institution that influenced the entire field of women's education in the Southwest. It was the most widely known private college of its type.

### Southern Born

Lucy Ann Thornton was born in Salvisa, Kentucky, on November 15, 1839. She was the middle child of three born to Willis Strother and Esther Stevens Thornton. Both parents came from families well known in the social and political life of the community. Lucy learned her southern charm and graciousness from her mother, a very feminine and religious woman. Young ladies of social standing attended private schools for their formal education. Lucy went to the Reverend Stuart Robinson's Institute in Georgetown, Kentucky. There she began her lifelong interest in literature, history, and the arts.

In 1856 nineteen-year-old Lucy married Dr. Henry Byrd Kidd, a thirty-six-year-old widower with no children. He was born in Kentucky but became a leading physician in Mississippi. He took his new bride to Yazoo

111

*Lucy Ann Thornton Kidd-Key*
—Courtesy Red River Historical Museum,
Sherman, Texas

City, Mississippi, a town surrounded by large plantations, including one owned by Jefferson Davis. Sarah,
Lucy's older sister, married Dr. W. Y. Gadberry and they
also moved to Yazoo City. Doctors Kidd and Gadberry
went into partnership and bought a pharmacy. Dr. Kidd
increased his wealth by buy-
ing other real estate.

> *"I have an
> abiding faith in
> the sanity of
> women."*
> — Lucy Ann
> Thornton
> Kidd-Key

Lucy led a very com-
fortable life with a house
full of servants. Her first
child, Sarah, was born in
1858 and Henry, Jr., was
born in 1860. Lucy's wid-
owed mother lived with
them. The two women were
active in the Methodist
church and local society.

**The Civil War**

The Civil War (1861-1865) ended the Kidds' life of
luxury. Following the war the aristocratic life of the South
had been destroyed. Plantations and businesses had been
burned. Federal troops camped on farmland, and carpet-
baggers took over unguarded property. Dr. Kidd sold off
land for money to live. Lucy helped make money by baking pies and selling them to the troops.

Their son, Price, was born during the turmoil of the
Civil War. When Edwin, another son, was born in 1870,
Dr. Kidd had difficulty supporting his large family, much
less regaining his wealth. Tragedy struck in 1873 with
the death of their son Price. Dr. Kidd's health then began

to deteriorate, and he was an invalid for years before his death in 1877.

Thirty-eight-year-old Lucy Kidd was widowed with three children to support. With a huge amount of debts, she could not wait for something to happen. She had to take action. Although she had no business experience to guide her, she began to recover the family's losses. First she filed suit for nonpayment on land Dr. Kidd had sold in 1876. The court ruled in her favor and she collected the money. She then sold land that she had inherited from her husband and began to collect long overdue pharmaceutical bills owed by regular customers. As soon as Kidd began to feel encouragement in the family's finances, another tragedy struck. Her oldest son, seventeen-year-old Henry, Jr., died while attending medical school in Kentucky.

**A Wise Investment**

A happy occasion for the widow was her only daughter's wedding. Sarah married Joseph H. Holt, a lawyer and justice of the peace, in 1878.

With the family finances stable, Kidd wanted an investment to secure some money. She investigated Whitmore College, a girls' school, in Brookhaven, Mississippi. The school had an excellent reputation for training young women.

Kidd bought an interest in Whitmore and became the proprietress of the Boarding Department. The president of Whitmore, Dr. H. F. Johnson, led the college through one of its biggest periods of expansion. Kidd learned about managing an educational institution from him. She also met Maggie Hill, a teacher, who became her closest lifelong friend. They believed that "education for girls must always give a large share of those things that enrich the personal life, that rightly motivate action and fix right standards of living in the home. To do those things is the special mission of art education."

Kidd's reputation as a champion for women's education in the arts grew during her tenure at Whitmore. She was praised for her contributions by Mississippi governor Robert Lowry. While Kidd was establishing her reputation in Mississippi, another girls' college was deteriorating in Sherman, Texas.

## A College President

Sherman Male and Female Academy was established on four acres of land in 1870. A two-story frame house was built on Post Oak Creek. The coeducational school lasted only a year before becoming the property of the North Texas Conference of the Methodist Episcopal Church, South. The boys were sent to another school and the academy was renamed North Texas Female College. The school had several presidents over the years, and the trustees basically ran the school. By 1887 the college was so in debt that the church closed it. For a year the buildings were empty and weeds and brush took over the once garden-like grounds.

Charles Galloway, the youngest bishop in the Methodist church, recommended that the North Texas Conference consider Lucy Ann Kidd to open the run-down school. Kidd traveled to Sherman in April 1888. The board was impressed with the southern lady and her educational credentials. They also thought she had money to help erase the debt owed by the college. While the college was valued at $15,000, it included an $11,000 debt for mortgages. The trustees thought she had enough money of her own to repair and open the campus. Kidd did not let them know that she had less than $10,000 to invest.

She accepted a ten-year contract to operate the school and agreed to have the dilapidated buildings ready to open in September, barely five months away. The *Sherman Daily Democrat* ran several articles about Kidd and her letters of recommendation from Bishop Galloway and the governor of Mississippi. She was described as "a Christian lady in every way calculated to fully meet the requirements of her."

## Staffing a College

Kidd's first act as president of North Texas Female College was to contact her friend, Maggie Hill, and offer her a teaching job. Then she returned to Brookhaven to resign her position there. She not only resigned, but hired four of Whitmore's best teachers to return to Sherman with her.

Edwin Kidd, an eighteen-year-old student at the University of Mississippi, withdrew and accompanied his mother to Sherman. He became the college secretary and financial agent. Kidd's daughter, Sarah, had studied music in New Orleans, New York, and Paris. Widowed with one daughter, Sarah moved to teach voice at her mother's school.

Traveling by coach and wagon, Kidd returned to

Sherman in July 1888 with her family and servants. She brought enough furniture to fill the vacant places in the school. Her money was sewn into her petticoat so no one would know how little she had.

Kidd hired contractors to repair the buildings and began recruiting students and seeking donations for the school. She traveled across Texas and the Indian Territory (now Oklahoma) to attend church sessions and camp meetings. Her trips were made on horseback and in stagecoaches in the scorching summer heat. Nothing deterred the determined, blue-eyed, five-foot-tall southern lady.

Not everyone agreed with Kidd's philosophy that educating women in the arts enriched their lives. Many thought education was wasted on girls who were meant to be wives and mothers. At one tent meeting she had to follow a minister who preached that music and musical instruments were tools of the devil. Few people in the audience responded to her plea for educating women in those skills. She did not become discouraged, though. She took advantage of her aristocratic background that boasted kinship to Jefferson Davis, John Marshall, James Madison, and Patrick Henry. It opened doors to the most influential and monied families.

**Building a Women's College**

North Texas Female College opened on time in September 1888. Kidd began her next campaign: to build more facilities. The school had only two buildings, a red brick chapel and a two-story frame house where classes were held. Out-of-town students boarded in neighborhood houses. Post Oak Creek, which ran through the four acres of campus, flooded with every heavy rain. Mud ran down the hill and slid into the ground floor of the classroom building. Kidd hired a landscape expert to improve the poorly drained grounds.

With a successful first year behind her, Kidd bought four adjoining lots with her own money. The expansion of the campus began with the building of Annie Nugent Hall, a three-story frame dormitory. It was the first of more than a dozen buildings constructed during Kidd's twenty-eight years as president. The chapel was enlarged and renamed for a benefactor. A building that housed the dining room and kitchen was built in 1897. Leona Kimbley Hall had six cottages for the faculty and Kidd's family plus an infirmary.

The school was the first in Texas to hire a nurse whose sole duty was to attend students. The library grew to over 1,000 volumes. The school catalog boasted that "This is the only woman's college in the State that has a *large* telescope, five *full concert grand* pianos, eighty uprights, and a well-equipped *chemical and physical laboratory.*"

### A New Marriage

Kidd had been a widow for almost fifteen years when she married Joseph Staunton Key. Key, a widower with three grown children, was a bishop of the Methodist church. Their wedding on April 5, 1892, created problems about Kidd's new name. She was known professionally as Mrs. Kidd. Although it was very bold and

118

unheard of at that time, she decided to hyphenate her name to Kidd-Key.

Kidd-Key did not conform to tradition in other ways. She was a mixture of the traditional and the practical. She taught her students that they were women and should always act womanly. But she added, "If a woman has brains, *and they all have,* let them think for themselves and not twine themselves helplessly about a man. We need more courageous women." She challenged parents to educate their daughters to be self-sufficient.

Kidd-Key set an example for her young women to follow. She dressed in the latest fashion of femininity. She preferred dresses with trains that made her seem taller. Her erect posture also added to the illusion of height. She was a mixture of romanticism, toughness, and efficiency. She showed all sides of her character to the students at North Texas Female College while upholding the school's rules.

## College Life

Students wore everyday clothes to class, but if they left the campus they had to wear the navy-blue uniform of the college. The young women never left campus unchaperoned unless they were accompanied by their parents. Some girls slipped down the fire escape. If they were caught, they were campused and could not leave the grounds of the school for a period of time. Dates were in chaperoned parlors only. The girls wrote a poem about their restrictions:

# SUGAR BABE

"Are maids heart-free
at old Kidd-Key?"
The answer with alarm,
"A watchman bold and brave (we're told)
Still guards them from all harm."

Kidd-Key purchased Mary Nash College, across the street from North Texas, and began the only conservatory of music in Texas. She hired a world-renowned pianist, Harold von Mickwitz, as director of the conservatory and brought in popular orchestras and singers to perform at the school. Students and faculty gave free concerts for Sherman residents.

## Financial Problems

By 1912 the college had reached its peak enrollment of five hundred students from fourteen states and Canada. But World War I brought a decline in enrollment. Social and financial conditions changed for the worse. Fewer scholarships were available, and many girls could no longer afford the tuition.

In 1915, Kidd-Key paid faculty salaries from her personal funds because of a $10,000 deficit in income. She refused to close the school although competition for students had grown. Young women wanted to be trained in the business world and saw their mission in life more than making a happy home for husbands and children.

The last class to receive a full degree graduated in 1916. Kidd-Key made plans with Edwin Kidd and Maggie Hill Barry to convert North Texas to an accredited junior college. Tired and dispirited, she left Edwin in charge of the change and went north for the summer to escape the summer heat. On her return trip to Sherman, she became ill and died in her home on September 13, 1916. North Texas had been opened as a junior college only one week earlier. People came from all over Texas to pay their respects to one of the leading educators of the time. The whole town of Sherman stopped all activities during her funeral at Travis Street Methodist Church.

Edwin Kidd became president of the college, with Sarah Holt Versel as vice-president. In 1919 the college changed its name to Kidd-Key College and Conservatory. The Methodist church bought the property from Kidd-Key's heirs in 1920, the year Bishop Joseph Key died at the age of ninety-one. The school could not survive money problems and closed during the Great Depression in 1935.

Lucy Ann Thornton Kidd-Key was a pioneer in women's education. She taught and lived her philosophy of life: "To live in the world you must be friends with people—else you can not do them any good."

*Jane Yelvington McCallum*

# JANE YELVINGTON McCALLUM
## 1878 -1957

Jane Yelvington McCallum could have been correctly called "Superwoman" during her lifetime. She led in the fight for women's suffrage and became the first female lobbyist in Texas. McCallum was committed to educational reform, prohibition, and reform of child labor laws. Governor Dan Moody appointed her as his secretary of state, the second woman to hold that office.

### A Native Texan

McCallum was born Jane LeGette Yelvington in La Vernia, Texas, on December 30, 1878. Jane's parents, Mary Fullerton LeGette and Alvaro Leonard Yelvington, married in 1874 and lived most of their lives in La Vernia, where at one time "bad men were as thick as flies." The young couple had six children. Jane was the oldest to survive and was spoiled because her brother died just three months before she was born. There were two sons and two daughters after Jane's birth.

Jane attended Wilson County schools and a Mississippi finishing school, Zealey's Female College. Her best friend, Mamie, married at age sixteen and left Jane very lonely. She wrote Mamie long letters about how she missed her and how strict her parents were about her dating.

> *"If a woman steals from her employer, does her father, husband, brother or son serve out her term in prison? . . . Why is it that the only place in the world a man wants to represent a woman is at the ballot box?"*
> — Jane Yelvington McCallum

**Marriage and Children**

Two years after she complained to her friend about marrying, Jane fell in love with Arthur Newell McCallum, principal of the La Vernia high school. On October 26, 1896, Jane, not quite eighteen years old, married McCallum, thirteen years older than she. The local newspaper announced the wedding and remarked that the couple was a perfect match. Jane was described as having a "beautiful face and figure," and McCallum was said to "hold the enviable reputation of being the embodiment of all that makes manhood honorable."

The McCallums' first child, Kathleen, was born in 1897, the year that Mr. McCallum was named superintendent of schools in Kenedy. The school was an eight-room, two-story building with no blinds on the windows and no piano for music. Jane decided to "establish a little theater" to raise money for the school. She knew nothing about drama besides taking parts in dramas when she was younger. But no one knew any more than she did, so she gathered together townspeople to perform: the banker's assistant, the hotel keeper, the baker, and the town belle. The plays were very successful and earned more than enough money to buy blinds and a piano for the school.

In 1900 their son Alvaro Yelvington was born, and Mr. McCallum accepted a job as superintendent of schools in Seguin. Their family grew with the births of Arthur Newell, Jr., in 1901, and Brown in 1903. Jane was expected to take part in afternoon teas and card parties where women discussed fashion, home decorations, and menus. To escape the boredom of such gatherings, Jane joined the Shakespeare Club. She met Ella Dibrell and together they formed a Village Improvement Society.

## Lobbying Begins

Jane, chairman of the Village Improvement Society, convinced property owners to plant trees. Then she persuaded the city fathers to water the trees so they would not die. The society raised enough money to build two large club rooms with folding doors. One was used as a meeting room and library. The second one was furnished with a maid who provided free babysitting so women could do their shopping on Saturdays.

When an opening was announced for a superintendent of public schools in Austin, Jane persuaded her husband to apply for the position. He was elected superintendent of the Austin public schools in 1903. He kept the same position until he retired in 1942. Jane was invited to join twenty-five clubs and societies after moving to Austin. With one maid, four children, and another on the way, she had neither the time nor the money to join the groups. What free time she could make for herself was spent pursuing her own interests. She joined the Shakespeare Club, researched her ancestors, and applied for membership in the Colonial Dames. She was accepted into the Texas Chapter of Colonial Dames in 1905.

Jane and her husband wrote a spelling book, *McCallum-Horn Speller,* in 1906. She selected the words and Mr. McCallum wrote the exercises and rules. Mr. Horn made no contribution, but his name was included on the speller. The speller was adopted by Texas schools as a textbook. The book brought extra money for the growing family. Henry, their fifth child, was born in 1907.

Jane enrolled at the University of Texas in 1912. She took courses in English composition and journalism through the spring of 1915. Her first publication, "The Builder of Formosa," about the sculptress Elisabet Ney, appeared in *The Texas Magazine* in October 1915.

### Suffrage Movement

Jane did not neglect her children or her husband, but she was critical of her position as a woman in society. She resented that women could not vote and were "politically classified with 'Idiots, Imbeciles, and the Insane.'" After Jane's father died, her mother lived with them and helped care for the children. That freed McCallum to devote time to the suffrage movement. In 1915 she was elected president of the Austin Women Suffrage Association. McCallum was a skilled organizer and a good writer. She led a door-to-door campaign to get more women to join the group, enlisting volunteers to address and mail information about the suffrage movement to Austin women. The group raised funds to finance their efforts with a play and a dance. She also lobbied the Democratic Convention delegates seeking support for suffrage. In 1916 the group changed its name to Texas Equal Suffrage Association.

On April 7, 1917, Congress declared war on Germany—the official beginning of World War I for America. The women's suffrage movement argued that if women could do men's jobs during the war, they should be able to vote. McCallum convinced the *Austin American* to run a weekly column, "Suffrage Corner," for several months before the suffrage bill was introduced in the legislature.

## Opposition

Texas Governor James E. Ferguson was opposed to women voters. Ferguson fired many professors at the University of Texas and was investigated for his management of public funds. Charged with twenty-one articles of impeachment, he was found guilty on ten of them. The Court of Impeachment convicted him by a vote of twenty-five to three.

Some legislators agreed with Ferguson about women voters. One anecdote that McCallum often told was of a visit to a Texas senator, who was not pleased to be interrupted by a woman.

"You ought to get married and tend to a woman's business," he barked at her.

"But I am married," she replied.

"Then you ought to be having children," he argued.

"I have five. How many do you suggest I have?" McCallum asked.

"Then you should be home taking care of them," the senator said irritably.

"They're in school and their grandmother is there in case they come home early," she replied.

"Then you should be home darning socks!" the senator blurted out.

## A Determined Lady

McCallum had a sense of humor, but she could be tough. It took courage for women to stand up against men of power. When a legislator told a group of suffragists that ladylike women would not want to vote, McCallum demanded, "You apologize and do it now!" The legislator immediately apologized.

Minnie Fisher Cunningham, state president of the Texas Equal Suffrage Association, asked McCallum to be a lobbyist for the suffrage cause. By January 1918 President Woodrow Wilson spoke in favor of an amendment to allow women to vote in all primary elections. With the help of Texas Governor William Pettus Hobby, the women's movement intensified their efforts. McCallum spoke to rural community women's groups to involve them in the fight.

The Primary Election Bill passed both houses and was signed into law by Governor Hobby on March 26, 1918. The suffrage leaders set up schools to teach women how to vote before the primary election in July. They circulated samples of ballots, studies of the issues, and candidates' records. By election day 306,000 Texas women were registered to vote. McCallum commented that the large number of registered women was "surely a convincing answer to the statement that 'Southern women do not want to vote.'" Women had won a victory in Texas, but they still could not vote in national elections.

### The Petticoat Lobby

McCallum expanded her column in the *Austin American* to "Women and Her Ways." By June 1918 she was writing "Women in Politics." The Equal Suffrage Association became the State League of Women Voters in 1919. They directed their efforts to getting Hobby reelected governor and Annie Webb Blanton named as superintendent of public instruction for the state of Texas.

The Nineteenth Amendment gave women across the nation the right to vote in all elections. In 1922 women's groups all over the state joined together to organize the Women's Joint Legislative Council. They were able to influence the Thirty-eighth Legislature to pass an emergency appropriation for public schools, revised and strengthened prohibition laws, and lobbied for a bill providing for a survey of conditions in Texas prisons, a bill for surveying the condition of public education, a provision for registering births, and federal assistance for the care of expectant mothers and newborn babies. Led by McCallum, they became known as "The Petticoat Lobby."

McCallum campaigned for Dan Moody for governor. He was running against Miriam "Ma" Ferguson, a front for her husband James E. Ferguson, who had been impeached as governor. When Moody defeated Miriam Ferguson, he appointed McCallum as secretary of state in 1924. Miriam Ferguson defeated Ross Sterling in the governor's race in 1932, and McCallum was out of a job. McCallum cautioned women "never vote for a woman just because she is a woman. . . . It is the candidate's platform which is important—not the battle of the sexes. . . ."

Before her death on August 14, 1957, Jane Yelvington McCallum summed up the reason for her tireless efforts to win women's right to vote when she wrote: "We asked for the vote as a right denied. We never said that women would improve the world, though in our hearts we believed it."

# PATRICIA MCCORMICK
## November 18, 1930 -

A TEXAS
FIRST
AS A
BULLFIGHTER

Patricia McCormick did what people told her a woman could not and should not do. She became the first North American woman bullfighter. She won the respect of the top full-fledged matadors with whom she fought, and was awarded many honors for her bravery.

### A Pretend Matador

Patricia McCormick was born on November 18, 1930, in St. Louis, Missouri. Her father was a civil engineer for an oil company. They had to move frequently because of his job. From St. Louis, they moved to Arkansas City, Kansas, on to Edwardsville, Illinois, and finally stopped in Big Spring, Texas, in 1943.

When McCormick was seven years old, her parents took her to Mexico for vacation. She saw her first bullfight and lost herself in the matadors' performances and the crowd's applause. The colorful arena was the stage for a great drama. She was fascinated by the matador's bravery in facing large black bulls with only a cape. She saw the movements of the man and bull as a beautiful dance. Her parents wanted to leave the arena, but McCormick wanted to stay. They disapproved of the whole idea of bullfighting and saw it as cruel and violent. She saw only the beauty of it.

*Patricia McCormick*
—Courtesy Patricia McCormick

132

The *corrida* (bullfight) became McCormick's favorite game when they returned home. She was always the matador. Her father was the bull as he mowed the yard and passed under her cloth. She got in trouble when she used the American flag for a cape. Her mother was upset that McCormick would put the flag to such "barbaric use." After she got in trouble again for using the tablecloth for a cape, she used an old blanket or her coat.

> *"I'm ambitious— not for fame and glory, but to master what I have to do; to reach the* cumbre, *as they say in bullfighting, the summit."*
> — Patricia McCormick

McCormick tried to use dogs and cats for a bull. Although the dogs were more cooperative than the cats, they just wanted to play with the cape. She even had a pet duck at one time, but it refused to pretend to be a bull. Her parents humored their only child in her pretend game, not understanding how serious she was about bullfighting.

## A Dreamer

McCormick was a romantic. She invented gypsies, matadors, and Robin Hood as her playmates. She spent a lot of study time creating stories in her own imagination. Her father told her, "Dreams are fine as long as you don't let them master you." When asked what she wanted to be when she grew up, she always said she wanted to be an

133

artist. But when McCormick was in Big Spring High School, she discovered gypsy songs and popular arias from operas. The romantic music added background for her fantasies of gypsies and matadors. She decided she wanted to be a musician.

## College Student

A young, unsophisticated Pat McCormick saw college as an adventure, a way of discovery. She entered the University of Texas in Austin in 1948. Against her mother's advice, McCormick chose to study music-drama in college. The comparison of bullfighting with music, drama, and art was always in her mind. She had a few friends who were *aficionados* (fans) of bullfighting. She studied all of the Spanish and Mexican bullfight magazines she could find. When her parents learned she was trying to get a cape, they were upset. They thought she had finally outgrown her bullfighting fantasies.

For a year she tried to make the best of her studies in music. She finally accepted that she did not have the voice for opera and no amount of work could change that. Since there were no classes in bullfighting, she changed her major to art. McCormick was shocked when a university counselor told her, "You have to get over wanting to be the best." At his advice she started her second year at the university as an art major, but she was not very happy. After many discussions with her parents, she was allowed to transfer to Texas Western in El Paso to study art with Urbici Soler, a well-known professor of sculpture and life drawing.

### Plaza de Toros

In February 1950 McCormick transferred to Texas Western. She was excited to be so close to a real *plaza de toros* (bullfighting arena). As soon as an opportunity presented itself, she attended a bullfight in Juarez, just across the U.S.-Mexico border from El Paso. After more than ten years of dreaming and pretending, McCormick saw her second bullfight. The wind was blowing and the cape was difficult to control. The fight was a disappointment, but she continued to return time and again. She watched closely to learn what made a good or bad bullfight.

Her first experience with a real cape came on April 2, 1950. Another Texas Western student, Julie Williams, also wanted to be a bullfighter, but her mother forbade her to do it. She took McCormick to meet Bullido, an old *banderillero* (one who places barbed sticks in the bull prior to the fight). Bullido showed McCormick the basic pass with the magenta and gold cape used in the first part of the bullfight. He showed her how to hold the cape with her hands and arms in the proper positions and pointed out her mistakes in swinging the cape. But in the end, Bullido refused to teach her.

She did not allow his refusal to dampen her spirits. She used an old blanket and practiced the basic movements for months in her dorm room, on campus, and on the tennis courts. She was more determined than ever to become a bullfighter. During her second year at Texas Western, she attended *aficionado* meetings and made friends with those interested in bullfighting. Her steady date, Tom, expressed an interest in bullfighting, but he believed it was not a profession for a woman.

135

McCormick's grades were not as good as her parents wished, so she convinced them to allow her to stay in El Paso for summer school. She did not tell them the real reason she wanted to stay. She wanted to be near the bullfights. McCormick was determined to find a good teacher and learn whether or not she was pursuing the impossible.

The editors of the school magazine asked McCormick to dress up as a matador and be photographed in the Juarez Plaza de Toros. She went to the chapel at the Juarez ring, where the matadors pray before a fight, and dedicated herself "to becoming a true *espada*" (swordsman). She prayed that the Virgin of Guadalupe would help her. When her picture appeared in the school publication, many of her friends teased her about being a bullfighter.

Some of the young men from the *aficionado* club went to the Juarez stockyards to cape bulls each Sunday. McCormick convinced a friend to take her along on a Sunday morning. There were wild bulls from the open range in a corral. McCormick was allowed to take a turn with a bull. The wild bull tossed her about a couple of times before he finally charged and she was able to pass him with a cape. She was so excited that she got him to charge the cape again before she was pulled from the corral.

Mr. Park Look had seen her picture and heard about her interest in bullfighting. He told her he thought she could be a professional and would like to sponsor her. Roberto Monroy, publicity head of the Juarez ring, presented her with her first cape, which had belonged to a famous matador. He also introduced her to Alejandro del Hierro, a retired matador with an excellent reputation. Del Hierro did not teach students who did not show talent or dedication to the profession. He told McCormick it would be a lot of hard work; she could not hope to fight professionally for a year or two.

## A Strict *Maestro*

Del Hierro agreed to become her *maestro*. She could not smoke, drink, or stay out late, and she had to do everything he told her to do. And she had to practice the same exercises day after day. One day as she was practicing, Roberto Gonzales, manager of the Plaza de Toros, asked her if she would like to do *quites* with an all-woman group of Mexican *matadoras* to be featured in the ring. (*Quites* are maneuvers to take the bull away from horse or man when either is in danger.) Del Hierro gave McCormick his permission to do it.

Her first experience on August 12, 1951, was not as successful as she had hoped. She was tossed three times by the bull's horns before she passed the bull successfully. But there was applause and music for her bravery. McCormick's friend Tom threatened to tell her parents about her bullfighting. She knew she had to tell them before they found out from someone else. Even though Mr. Look explained to them that she had a lot of talent, they were very angry. They decided to drive to El Paso to confront her. After they met Mr. Look and Alejandro del Hierro and saw her determination, they reluctantly agreed to give their permission for her to give bullfighting a try.

## The Bullfight

Bullfighting is founded upon "the bravery of the bull, its savagery, its desire to charge." The bulls that fight in the ring are a special breed called *toros de lidia*

137

(bulls of combat). Ranches are devoted exclusively to the breeding and handling of the wild bulls. Matadors and *novilleros* are invited to the ranch to test the bull's bravery at two years old. Then the bulls are turned loose in the wild range for another two years and see no man on foot until they are in the arena for the fight. The huge, black bulls are suitable only for the bullring and are born with a primal instinct to use their horns to kill anything that disturbs them.

There is a ritual to a bullfight. Prior to the fight there is an announcement of an "Appointment with Death" through posters or newspaper articles and advertisements. The bullfight is divided into *tercios* (thirds). The changing of the *tercios* is signaled by the blowing of a bugle in the stands of the judge. Tension mounts as each *tercio* begins. In the first *tercio* there is a grand parade honoring the Virgin of Macarena, who protects the bullfighters. The matadors bow to the honored guests, and the ring is cleared for the bull's appearance. While the matador watches, assistants cape the bull to see how it reacts. Then there is the placement of the *vara* (a pointed shaft) in the bull's shoulders to lower its head. The second *tercio* is the placement of *banderillas* (barbed, decorated sticks) to correct the carriage of the bull's head. The third is the *tercio* of the death, where the bull is killed after the matador shows his skill and bravery with the cape. Killing the bull is the climax. The matador can be awarded nothing, an ear, two ears, tail, or foot at the discretion of the judge. The judge can be influenced by the crowd waving white handkerchiefs and applauding.

138

## Appointment with Death

McCormick had her first appointment with death on September 9, 1951. On the day of the fight she prayed in the chapel of Plaza de Toros, a ritual for all bullfighters, before the pageantry of the afternoon began. In the *tercio* of the death, McCormick faced Ferdinando, a two-and-half-year-old bull, which charged into the ring like a conqueror. She did cape passes from the side and then passes where she faced the bull with the cape to her side, which required great bravery. During her work with the cape, she was knocked down once before she asked permission for the kill. She held the *muleta* (small red cape) and sword too high, and on the third pass the bull caught her with a horn and threw her on its back. She thrilled the crowd with her recovery and bravery in facing the bull again. When she made a good kill, the music blared and the people stood and cheered. She was awarded an ear for her performance.

Newspapers printed stories about the first North American woman bullfighter. One writer described her as being "tall and slim, with almost no hips" and remarked that her "honey blond hair and blue eyes" made her stand out in the ring. Another reporter wrote of her first kill, "When she is working coolly and not in trouble, she gets the feeling of art that all great *toreros* have. Some call it emotion. At any rate she's got it."

Alejandro del Hierro told her if she wanted to be in the category of matador there were several things she had to do. First, she had to become a *novillera* and fight in a specific number of fights. She had to be accepted into the Union of *Matadors* and *Novilleros* and win the approval of the hard-to-please fans in the Plaza Mexico in Mexico City.

139

## Baptism of Blood

McCormick became a union member with the official title of *Matadora de Novillos-Toros*. The union required her to fight on the same standards with the same regulations of a professional matador. She was the only female member and alternated with men on equal terms. Her professional career as a bullfighter began on January 20, 1952, in Juarez, Mexico. For a year she and Del Hierro traveled from one first-class bullring to another, with stops at ranches to test bulls between fights. She had her "baptism of blood" on January 14, 1953, while testing cows at La Punta, a famous bull ranch in Mexico. She was gored in the thigh and could not walk for several days nor work again for over four weeks.

She received both praise for her bravery and criticism for her foolishness. One of her strongest critics was Tom Lea, author of *The Brave Bulls*. He disapproved of McCormick because, he said, "women should not associate with death." Many people questioned why she risked her life fighting bulls. She explained that as she started into the ring she became two persons: "the one I am inside, the flame that makes me do this thing which is strange for a woman and for an Anglo-Saxon, and another person who smiles at people and walks erect and guards the inside person and the flame and the feelings."

Her "baptism of blood" did not put out the flame that burned inside her. She suffered many wounds and six major gorings during her career, including a serious one in Tijuana in 1954, a nearly fatal one in Acuña in 1955, and another serious one in Caracas, Venezuela, in 1959. She was so badly injured in Acuña that a priest gave her last rites, but any single goring could have ended her career.

McCormick maintained top billing from 1952 to 1962, when she retired from the bullring. She fought approximately 300 bullfights during her career, alternating between two popular matadors. Sometimes she killed as many as three bulls in an afternoon. There was one exception to her fighting with men only. She starred with Juanita Aparecio, Mexico's finest *matadora,* in Venezuela.

She was not permitted to become a *matador de alternativa,* the formal ceremony of becoming a full-fledged matador. *Alternativas* were not permitted to be given to women during her time. Had she taken *alternativa,* full-fledged matadors would not have fought with her even though she had been fighting with them as one. Also, she could not have fought with *novilleros.* Her career would have been cut short for lack of bullfights.

McCormick's greatest obstacle was not facing the bulls, but it was overcoming the prejudice against women bullfighters. A famous matador said about McCormick, "Had she not been born a woman, she might have been better than any of us." But McCormick did not see it that way. She said, "Bullfighting has no frontier. It depends upon the individual—not the sex. It has been a man's profession formerly because of the life itself."

Patricia McCormick retired to California in 1962 to teach and pursue her art. She is still following her own advice: "Follow your goals and passions. Don't be afraid to make mistakes."

*Irma Rangel*

—Courtesy Irma Rangel

# IRMA L. RANGEL
## May 15, 1931 -

A TEXAS
FIRST
AS A
HISPANIC
LEGISLATOR

Irma Rangel was the first Mexican-American woman elected to the Texas House of Representatives, the Mexican-American Legislative Caucus, and the first Mexican-American to be the chairperson of the House Committee of Higher Education. She opened doors for many women when she attended law school at St. Mary's University at a time when it was discouraged as a profession for women.

## Hooky Player

Irma Rangel played hooky on her first day of school. She did not know she was playing hooky because she did not speak English and her teacher did not speak Spanish. When the teacher sent the students outside for recess, Irma went home. She thought it was the end of the school day. Someone called her mother and she took Irma back to school and explained about recess.

Irma attended Stephen F. Austin Elementary School, an all-Mexican-American school. The majority of students in Irma's "low zero" class spoke only Spanish. The students were divided into "low zero" and "high zero" groups. The zero level later became known as kindergarten. All of the grades were divided into low and high groups. Most of the students spoke only Spanish, but

Anglo teachers taught in English. There were only two Mexican-American teachers who taught in the fourth, fifth, and sixth grades. They taught in English, also, because no one was allowed to speak Spanish in school.

Irma's first years in school were very difficult. If the children forgot and spoke in Spanish, they were punished. One of her teachers had a paddle with holes in it and spanked the palms of Irma's hands when she spoke Spanish. She did not tell her parents when she was punished at school. If she or her older sisters, Olga and Minnie, were punished at school, they were punished again at home.

*"We grew up so accustomed to racial discrimination, I don't think it ever occurred to us to think that we were also being discriminated against as women."*
—Irma Rangel

This introduction to the English language was unarguably harsh, but Irma persevered. She and her sisters taught their parents English as they learned it. Irma learned quickly enough to be double promoted in elementary school.

## A Close Family

Irma was born in Kingsville, Texas, on May 15, 1931, to Mexican- American parents who spoke very little English. Her father, Presciliano M. Rangel, was orphaned at the age of five and was raised by his sisters.

He did not finish first grade. Her mother, Herminia (Minnie) Lerma, was orphaned at the age of eleven and raised by her brothers. Mrs. Rangel attended the Mexican Ward (later named the Stephen F. Austin Elementary School) through fifth grade. Mrs. Rangel's father was a ranch foreman at the El Jongo and Palo Alto ranches. He also rented cotton land and farmed. The family lived outside of Kingsville. When Irma's mother went to school, she had to pass a school where Anglo children attended. She was not allowed to go there and walked over a mile and a half to attend the Mexican Ward. The schools were still segregated when Olga, Minnie, and Irma attended the same school, only Mexican Ward was called Austin Elementary.

**Progressive Parents**

The older Rangels were ahead of their time. They were very aggressive and progressive. Mr. Rangel worked for a man who owned a barber shop. The barber taught Mr. Rangel how to cut hair. He became so well known for his work that when the owner wanted to sell the business, he bought the barber shop. He added another barber shop in Robstown, about twenty miles from Kingsville. He also started a dry cleaners and an appliance store. Then he bought a ranch with some farm land. Later, he started the Black Cat saloon with a pool hall upstairs and kitchen for making hamburgers on the same floor as the bar. Mr. Rangel also encouraged his wife to be independent, which was unusual for a man during the 1930s.

Mrs. Rangel wanted to start her own business, so

she opened a dress shop in their house. Each Sunday Mr. Rangel helped her load her stock of dresses in the car to peddle her wares. Olga, Minnie, and Irma took turns going with her to sell candy to the children while their mother sold dresses to the women. Mrs. Rangel drove to the farms surrounding Kingsville to sell to the farm wives who could not go to Kingsville to shop. She named her dress shop "The Three Sisters" after her three daughters. After the Rangels became financially successful, Mr. Rangel built a building which had room for The Three Sisters. Mrs. Rangel added other merchandise and the store became a department store instead of just a dress shop.

**Education**

Mr. and Mrs. Rangel stressed the importance of education to Olga, Minnie, and Irma. They were determined that their children take advantage of all educational opportunities. They encouraged their daughters to believe in themselves, and instilled in the girls a great love and great pride about being Mexican-Americans. They loved what and who they were, and they shared that love with their daughters.

Olga and Minnie were in high school when the first junior high school opened. Irma's class was the first to attend the new school. It was her first experience to share a school with Anglo-American students. The Mexican-American students were not accepted by the Anglo-Americans. Irma and her friends stayed to themselves. They were still punished if they were caught speaking Spanish at school.

High school was tougher for Irma. There were no

146

fights, but there were arguments about "their ignorance of Mexican-Americans and our ignorance about Anglo-Americans." Although the Anglos did not want to share their school with the Mexican-Americans, Irma overcame some of her own prejudice as well as theirs and participated in activities. She belonged to the Future Teachers of America, and was honored as one of the outstanding players on the girls' basketball team. Her sisters had also excelled in soccer and tennis when they were in high school. Because Irma was double promoted in elementary school, she graduated from high school just two weeks before her seventeenth birthday.

## Duty and Service

Along with pride in their heritage, Mr. and Mrs. Rangel instilled in their daughters a sense of duty and service to those less fortunate than they. Olga, Minnie, and Irma all chose to enter areas of public service. The oldest of the three, Olga Rangel (Lumley), became a teacher and earned her master's degree in education. The second, Minnie Rangel (Henderson), earned a degree in pharmacy at the University of Texas in Austin. She was the first Mexican-American woman pharmacist. She opened her own drugstore in Kingsville and often filled prescriptions free of charge to the poor.

Mr. and Mrs. Rangel wanted Irma to go into business administration, but Irma was determined to become a teacher. After she earned her teacher's certificate at Texas A&I in Kingsville, she taught in Robstown and Alice. At the age of twenty-five she was employed by an oil company to teach American children in Venezuela,

South America. She taught both Spanish and English before becoming a principal her last year with the oil company. In 1964 she went to Menlo Park, California, where she wrote a book, *How to Teach Spanish in the Elementary Grades,* while she was teaching.

## Back to School

In the summer of 1966 she returned to Kingsville. After fourteen years of teaching, she knew what she wanted to do. She wanted to study law. It had been her secret dream since she met Gus Garcia, a lawyer from San Antonio. She had never told her parents that she wanted to be a lawyer, being afraid they would say, "See, you didn't do it." They were thrilled when she told them she wanted to go to law school.

With her parents' financial support, Rangel moved to San Antonio in September 1966 to enroll in law school at St. Mary's University. St. Mary's had just become coeducational. In the past it had been an all boys' school. When she went to register, she was asked if she had taken the Law School Admissions Test (LSAT). She did not know what they were talking about. Only two other girls had enrolled: one part-time student (a Mexican-American) and one full-time (an Anglo-American). The registrar allowed Rangel to enroll with the understanding that she would take the LSAT in October.

Rangel was thirty-five years old and had been out of school for fourteen years. She had forgotten how to study and her concentration span was short. She had to read something two or three times before she understood it. The vocabulary was different. She had to look up everything in the dictionary. After two weeks, she was ready to drop out of law school. "I am not going to be the first dropout in my family," she told herself. She had to work hard, but she continued her studies.

In October she took and passed the LSAT. "Nothing is easy in life," she said. "You make a lot of sacrifices but you are rewarded for you sacrifices." Rangel earned a doctorate in jurisprudence and general practice in May 1969.

## Practicing Law

After she graduated from St. Mary's, she worked as a law clerk for Judge Adrian Spears in San Antonio. When she was offered a job as assistant district attorney in Corpus Christi, she refused until they offered her the same salary as the men in the same position. A little over a year later she joined the Canales and Garza law firm. It was during her three years in Corpus Christi that she became aware of the plight of young unwed mothers and the problems of juvenile delinquency in South Texas.

In 1973, Rangel and Hector Garcia, a Kingsville native, opened a law practice a block from Minnie Rangel Henderson's pharmacy. Rangel's father, mother, and sister told people about the firm. Rangel and Garcia gave an open house and invited people to visit their offices. Rangel accepted every invitation to speak so people would know that she was knowledgeable about the law. "But still, the first six months not even the flies would come in," she recalled with a laugh.

Although they did not intend to specialize, they found themselves handling worker's compensation claims.

Many Mexican-American workers did not realize they could be compensated by worker's compensation insurance when they were hurt until someone explained the process to them. Hector Garcia was very good in criminal law, but the first six months were very difficult for the only Mexican-American lawyers in Kingsville. Few Anglo-Americans would hire them. Ninety-five percent of their clients were Mexican-Americans.

## Politics

Rangel and Garcia had vowed that they would not become involved in politics when they set up their office in Kingsville. But Rangel had always been involved in one way or another since her return from South America. In 1966 she had marched in the farm workers' protest against mistreatment by the landowners. She was outspoken in her criticism of social welfare programs that did not aid untrained mothers with children to support. She was critical of education that favored one group over another in South Texas schools. She finally agreed to run as chairperson of the Kleberg County Democratic Party. She won the election with the help of her father, mother, and sister, who were well known and respected in the community.

In 1974 Rangel was invited to attend the LBJ School for Public Affairs Conference on Women in Public Life in Austin. The conference was led by Liz Carpenter and Lady Bird Johnson. There were no Mexican-American women among the speakers at the conference. The conference convinced Rangel that Mexican-American women had to become more involved in politics.

She decided to run for the Democratic House seat from District 49. Four candidates were running for the one position: one Anglo-American woman, two Mexican-American men, and Rangel. There was a runoff between Rangel and Jean K. Hines of Rivera, who had the support and financial backing from the King Ranch. Rangel won a close victory over Hines, and that is when "[she] suddenly realized what a great responsibility [she] had assumed."

**A First For Women**

Rangel did not know until she arrived at the Capitol in Austin that she was the first Mexican-American to be elected to the House of Representatives. She felt that she carried a burden because "whatever [she] said or whatever [she] did was going to reflect on the next Mexican-American woman." Rangel was tough-skinned and did not give in to the men if she disagreed.

An incident that stands out in her and her colleagues' minds happened during a debate in 1977. Rangel pushed to provide more money for indigent women and their children. There was so much noise on the floor that no one was listening. Suddenly, a lightbulb exploded with a loud *pop*. Everyone grew very quiet.

"Hey, someone up there is trying to send a message to you guys . . . Support this amendment," she said. The bill passed.

That was only one of the many bills introduced by Representative Rangel. She considers one of her greatest achievements the introduction of House Bill 1755, designed to provide employment and educational programs

151

for mothers with dependent children. Education and employment, especially among women and minorities, still remain high on her list of priorities.

In twenty-one years, Rangel has served as chair or vice-chair on many legislative committees, including chair of the Teacher Retirement System Insurance Subcommittee, chair of the Higher Education Committee, and elected chair of the Mexican-American Legislative Caucus. She also served on the Interim Committee for Mental Health and Mental Retardation. She has received many honors including being inducted into the Texas Women's Hall of Fame by Governor Ann Richards.

As a twenty-one-year veteran in the state legislature, she said, "I think I've gained the members' respect and set a good example for Mexican-American women in Texas." She hopes in the future she can look back and say, "I was only the first."

One of Irma Rangel's goals is "to convince students, especially Mexican-American students, that if they accept a sense of responsibility, they will have the same opportunities that I have. As Mexican-Americans, we have to work hard and educate ourselves well."

# ELIZABETH MARION WATSON
## August 25, 1949 -

Elizabeth M. Watson was the Houston Police Department's first female captain and its first female deputy chief. When she became Houston's chief of police, she was the first woman to head a police force in a city with a population greater than one million.

### A Shy Child

Elizabeth "Betsy" Herrmann was born in Philadelphia, Pennsylvania, on her mother's birthday, August 25, 1949. She was the second of six children born to John and Elizabeth Herrmann. Her older sister was the leader of the two and did everything for her. She protected the painfully shy Betsy, who avoided daring situations.

Mrs. Herrmann was a traditionalist who raised her children to make a contribution to society. Betsy learned a lot about life listening to her mother talk while they folded diapers. Her mother talked about the importance of family, of loving and taking care of each other. Mrs. Herrmann insisted that her children use proper pronunciation and grammar. She also encouraged them to be good readers.

Betsy always enjoyed outdoor activities and played with her brothers and sisters in the street of their Phila-

*Elizabeth Marion Watson*
—Courtesy Elizabeth Marion Watson

delphia suburb. Most of the time, her siblings protected her because she was so shy that she would not take up for herself. There was a large neighborhood boy who picked on her. Betsy started biting him every chance she got. One day Mrs. Herrmann showed her teeth to Betsy. Her mother asked her, "Do you know how much it would hurt if I were to bite you?" Betsy never bit anyone again.

> *"Do not become discouraged or disgruntled when there are signs of adverse impact on women; when there seem to be doors of opportunity that close; when there are signs of chauvinism being alive and well."*
> —Elizabeth Marion Watson

### An Invisible Student

Betsy attended Incarnation of Our Lord Catholic School. The nuns were very sensitive to her shyness, although she tried to be invisible in the classroom. Unless she was assigned a seat, she always tried to get in the back row. Betsy never volunteered to answer questions even when she knew the answers. She lived in dread that the teacher would call on her and she would have to speak in front of her classmates.

When she was in fifth grade, her teacher asked her to go to another classroom and borrow chalk. She was terrified that she could not do the task assigned to her. Before she got halfway between the classrooms, she had forgotten what she was sent to get. Then she had to decide whether to go on or return to the classroom empty-handed. As she stood frozen in her steps, another teacher rescued her from having to make the decision. As she was promoted from one class to another, understanding teachers gave her different tasks to perform, trying to bring her out of her shyness.

In 1963, John Herrmann, an aerospace physicist, was transferred to Houston, Texas, to work for the National Aeronautics and Space Administration (NASA). He was a project manager on the Apollo moon landing program. Mr. Herrmann reassured all of his children "that [they] could do anything [they] wanted to do. [They] were as smart as anyone [they] would meet in [their] lifetimes." It took Betsy a long time to understand what her father was trying to teach them.

**Texas Drawl**

Betsy was fourteen when her family moved to Houston, where she attended public schools. The transition from Philadelphia to Houston was traumatic for a still shy Betsy. She had never gone from one class to another and spent the first week being lost in the hallways. She almost failed algebra because she could not understand her teacher's Texas accent. She became so focused on listening to words that she missed the concepts. Betsy had never heard of a class schedule before. It was referred to as an "agenda" in the private school. When she was told to come to "after school make-up" and did not show up, her parents were called in for a conference. She thought "make-up" referred to cosmetics. When they realized the

156

problem, her sister began tutoring her in vocabulary and algebra. By the second semester she was making good grades again.

As a child, Betsy thought she wanted to be a nun. She saw the life of a nun as being serene, protected, and one of service. After she graduated from Jesse Jones High School in 1967, her father advised her to take a variety of courses in college before she made a career choice. When she entered Texas Tech University at Lubbock, she took a number of courses in the sciences. Botany was her favorite course, but there was no place in Texas to earn a degree in that area. The closest subject would have been in oceanography, which was offered at Texas A&M University at College Station. But Texas A&M did not allow female students at that time. Betsy decided to major in psychology. Although she graduated with honors in 1971, few jobs were available.

## A Family Tradition

Betsy's grandfather and uncles were police officers in Philadelphia. Her parents saw policing as a protected environment for their shy daughter because women were restricted in their assignments. They thought she would be shielded from physical confrontations and danger. Mrs. Herrmann convinced her daughter that police work might be an exciting way to use her psychology degree. Betsy joined the Houston Police Department in 1972, thinking that it was just temporary until she could find a "real job."

When she joined the department, there were two divisions where women were assigned: the juvenile center and the jail. Betsy entered the force at the lowest level of police work, the juvenile center. She did not wear a uniform and often was not recognized as a police officer. One of her duties was investigative work, so she was exposed to crimes committed by juveniles. But when she was assigned to the jail, she wore a uniform and was in constant contact with prisoners. Some of her duties included booking and searching prisoners, and assigning and accompanying them to cells. She also took them for court appearances and family or attorney visits.

Betsy thought she would quit after her tour in the juvenile center and jail, but she had an opportunity to go into criminal intelligence. When she was in her early twenties, she was an undercover cop and played roles to convince dealers of weapons and drugs that she was one of them. She said, "Playing a dumb brunette is not my idea of fun." Each time she experienced burn-out in an area, Betsy was promoted to a more challenging job. Her assignment in the homicide department was the most stressful of her assignments. The magnitude of daily violence took an emotional toil on her. She began having nightmares, reliving everything she had seen that day.


**Shyness Disappears**

During college and her first years of policing, Betsy began losing her shyness. She became aware of the change while being questioned by a very aggressive lawyer in a criminal case. The defense attorney began badgering her on a point of her testimony. He tried to confuse her to get her to make a contradictory statement. She became very angry, regained her composure, and spoke with authority. Her shyness seemed to have disappeared.

Betsy met Robert Lloyd "Chase" Watson in 1973 when they were both assigned to the jail. It was not love at first sight, but they started dating a few months later. They were married on June 18, 1976. There were so many police officers at the wedding reception that they had a sign for the officers to hang their guns at the door, "just like the old West." Their wedding day was also the day that Betsy was promoted to detective.

Betsy Watson was a traditionalist when she joined the police department. She never questioned anything because that was the way it had always been done. Over the years, though, she became more confident and began challenging some of the ideas that had always been accepted. She worked long hours, arriving early and staying late. Her intense motivation drew attention to her.

## Overcoming Prejudice

In the early 1980s, Watson was told that she could not be a supervisor in an investigative division because it was "too tough a job for a woman." She did not file a job-bias complaint, saying "My sense was that if I were to throw a tantrum, it probably wouldn't be an effective strategy. Catching flies with honey was a better approach."

Although her husband was happy with his status, he pushed Watson to compete for every promotion. When she was transferred out of the burglary division because she was a woman, she took the civil service exam for lieutenant. The promotion in rank made her one of the top

two women in the department. She volunteered to super-
vise the night shift at one of the toughest substations.

There was a lot of hissing and booing when it was
announced that Watson would be the lieutenant in
charge. Although it was tough at first, the men gradually
accepted her because she worked so hard. By the
mid-1980s Lee Brown, Houston's first black police chief,
recognized Watson's ability and began grooming her as a
future police chief. When he resigned in 1990 to become
police commissioner in New York City, Deputy Chief
Betsy Watson was one of a few who had the qualifica-
tions to take the job.

**Through the Ranks**
Over a period of seventeen years, Watson had gone
through the ranks, from a rookie police officer to serving
as commander of the auto thefts and inspection division.
She commanded a night shift patrol division and super-
vised the record division. She was also a detective in homicide, burglary and theft, and sex crimes for five years.
For a short time, Watson was even a member of the SWAT
team and served as head of Houston's West Side Command Station. The only thing she had not done was patrol
the streets, but that was only because she was a woman.

Still, Watson was hesitant to announce her candidacy for police chief. She felt that anyone who followed
Brown was doomed for failure. Brown had been a very
popular chief, but police morale was low and community
tensions were high. The officers had not had a raise in
five years, the department had taken five hundred officers off the streets, and there had been two highly controversial shootings of blacks by white officers. In addi-

tion, Watson had two young children and the promotion would mean personal sacrifice for her family. There was also the question of whether male officers would accept a woman as police chief. Watson told Mayor Kathryn Whitmore, Houston's first female mayor, "It is an awesome responsibility and a tremendous personal sacrifice, and I'm just not that noble."

## Top Gun

Mayor Whitmore would not take no for an answer and appointed Watson to the position in January 1990. Watson became the first female police chief in a city of over one million people. When she took the job she knew there were challenges. One of the things she did not expect, however, was to learn she was pregnant after only three months in the office. Watson's first thought was, "The community is going to say, 'That's what you get when you put a woman in the job.'"

She worried needlessly. If anyone made snide remarks, she did not hear them. She continued to work long hours, just as she did when she was pregnant with her other two children, Susan (1981) and Mark (1985). Her husband, who was very supportive, and brothers and sisters who lived nearby juggled schedules to help fill in for her. When David was born in December 1990, Watson took a six-week maternity leave. During that time her secretary brought work to her every day, and she attended important meetings at the department. She also spent a lot of time on the telephone.

## City Politics

During Watson's tenure, she appointed the first minority officer to serve on the police chief's command staff, established a Community Outreach Division to encourage citizens to get involved in policing issues, and got a salary increase for the police department. But the office of chief of police was a political position, an appointment by the mayor. In 1992, Kathryn Whitmore was defeated in the mayoral election by Bob Lanier. Watson was demoted to assistant chief, and Lanier appointed a new chief. Watson resigned and said she was glad to have been a police chief "partly because it was well worth doing and partly because I'll never have to do it again."

But Watson was soon approached to accept the position of chief of police in Austin. When she talked to her family about moving to Austin, eleven-year-old Susan said, "I don't care where we live as long as I can tell people that you are chief of police." It was a difficult decision because all of Watson's family lived in her [Houston] neighborhood. She had always been able to count on them for help and support, and they were the Watsons' best friends.

Watson changed her mind about never being chief of police again and accepted the job in Austin. After five years as chief of the Austin Police Department (1992-1997), she left to become a visiting fellow at the Office of Community-Oriented Policing, U.S. Department of Justice. Her job is to research police leadership and define the different levels of leadership roles. Her goal is to produce a model for police leadership development.

Watson sees it as an opportunity to make a national impact on policing as opposed to an impact on one community.

Her advice for women who want to enter law enforcement is "to get into the field. Every woman has to do the very best she can, so that it's easier for the next woman, and at the same time our whole profession [law enforcement] will be better served." Elizabeth Marion Watson has set the example for women who want to enter the ranks of law enforcement in Texas.

*Judith Zaffirini*

—Courtesy Judith Zaffirini

# JUDITH ZAFFIRINI
## February 13, 1946 -

Judith Zaffirini is the first Hispanic woman senator in Texas. She is the first to serve as president pro tempore of the Texas Senate and as Texas Governor for a Day. She carried all counties in the 21st Senatorial District to give her three landslide victories, something no one else has done. She is the only senator in the history of Texas with career-long 100 percent attendance and 100 percent voting records.

**A Funny Name**

Judy Pappas learned early to take teasing about her Greek name. The Spanish word for potato is *papas* and is pronounced the same as Judy's last name. "Here come Pappas and her Frito friends!" the boys teased. Another would sneak up behind her, give her a bear hug and say, "I like mashed potatoes." Still another would run up to her and ask, "Judy Pappas, can I have a bite?" She learned early to ignore teasing about her name.

Judith Pappas was born in Laredo, Texas, on the U.S.-Mexico border on February 23, 1946. She is the third of four daughters born to George Santiago Pappas of Greek descent and Nieves Mogas Pappas of Mexican-American descent. Mr. and Mrs. Pappas taught their daughters the importance of a loving family relationship and a deep-rooted religious faith. Mr. Pappas, a politically active railroad clerk, taught them a sense of politics. Judy took part in her first political campaign when she was five years old, calling people to remind them to vote.

> *"I have experienced prejudice as a Mexican-American with an Italian last name, as a woman and as a Catholic. I understand it for what it is. It reflects ignorance, lack of education, lack of experience."*
> —Judith Zaffirini

Judy started at St. Peter's School a year early because she cried to go to school with her sisters. After she began second grade, she told her mother she did not want to go to school again. Her mother allowed her to stay home from school the next day. She had to help her mother clean house all day, without complaining or playing. She went back to school the next day, having learned the value of education.

**Falling in Love**

Judy was in fifth grade when she fell in love. Her parents, younger sister, and Judy stopped at a local drugstore for some purchases. Her parents warned the girls to stay in the back seat of the car and not to touch anything. As soon as Mr. and Mrs. Pappas were inside the drugstore, Judy climbed over the seat and started moving anything that would move. The car was parked on an incline and started rolling backward toward a busy intersection. Two seventh-grade boys saw what was happening. One of them ran to the car and managed to stop it before it reached the intersection. The young man was Carlos Zaffirini. It was love at first sight for Judy, but it took Carlos several years to fall in love with her. She was too young!

Judy was a freshman at Ursuline Academy before Carlos, a junior at St. Joseph's Academy, noticed her. She was class cheerleader, class princess, class president, and president of the Student Council. She was having a wonderful time—but she was making all Fs in her classes. Carlos was a straight-A student. After they started dating, and he found out about her Fs, he told her, "If you do not straighten out, I will break up with you."

## A New Outlook

Judy turned her life around. She took her studies seriously and with Carlos' help, ended the year with all As except in algebra. At the end of the first nine weeks of her sophomore year, the principal of the school gave a blue and gold bow to every student with an A average. After she had given out all but one of the bows, she said, "I have held this one bow out because when you hear who it is for, you are not going to believe it. Judy Pappas!" There was a shocked pause and then the students began to laugh and applaud. The principal continued, "And the moral of the story is: If Judy Pappas can do it, *anybody* can."

Her activities did not stop with making the honor roll. When she was a junior, she was one of the founders of the Laredo High Hope Volunteers, who worked with mentally retarded people. There were few services for those persons and many could not afford medical care. Judy led fund drives to raise money to provide medications and medical care for the needy.

**Marriage**

Judy followed Carlos to the University of Texas in Austin after she graduated from high school. She had to drop out of school because of an illness her doctor labeled as terminal. She and Carlos, a law student, decided to get married in 1965 although she was only eighteen. "There have been many blessings in my life. Not only did I recover, but I ended up getting three degrees after I got married," she said.

Carlos finished UT Law School while Judy earned a BA and master's degree. (She later earned her doctorate in communications.) They worked their way through college by joining the staffs of state politicians. Judy worked for Texas Senator Wayne Connally and also for the Texas Department of Mental Health-Mental Retardation. One of Carlos' jobs was on the staff of Governor John Connally.

**Politics**

Judith Zaffirini taught communications at Laredo Junior College when they returned to Laredo in 1970. Her husband established his legal practice and they became involved in land development and ownership of a small mall. Their experiences in Austin gave them a strong interest in politics. They were active in state campaigns, but Zaffirini did not become interested in running for office until much later. "I saw, from the inside as a staff member, how some legislators walked [out] on

168

votes. I was very negatively impressed. I thought it was irresponsible that they wouldn't take a stand," she said. In 1978 Zaffirini moved into a leadership role in the Democratic Party with her election to the State Democratic Executive Committee (SDEC).

## A "Little Blessing"

After seventeen years of marriage and four miscarriages, Zaffirini gave birth to Carlos, Jr., in 1982. That "little blessing is the biggest blessing of all," she said. She did not allow her active life to interfere with parenting. Her motto has always been "to prioritize my work, and my priority has been the same for years—faith and family first, and business and politics later."

In 1984 she was elected as vice-chairman of the Texas Democratic Party. She was the highest ranking woman and the highest ranking Hispanic in the state party. Suggestions that she run for the Texas Senate had begun to surface in 1983 and picked up momentum by 1985. She began to ask friends their opinions to help make the decision.

The decision to run for the Senate stopped with the TWA hostage crisis. Mr. and Mrs. Vincente Garza, old and close friends of Zaffirini, were among the hostages of Muslim extremists in Beirut. Zaffirini led arrangements for a prayer vigil at Blessed Sacrament Catholic Church. Only after the safe return of the Garzas did she resume her interest in the race for senator. Her family and friends encouraged her to run, and Vincente Garza became her campaign treasurer.

## On the Campaign Trail

Judith Zaffirini's opponent in the 1986 election was State Representative Billy Hall. Retiring Senator John Traeger endorsed Hall. Zaffirini refused to be labeled a liberal or a conservative, saying she would vote on the issues. She pledged to find ways to provide for the social and economic security of the family. She refused special interest money to run her campaign, and instead depended on volunteers which included her mother, father, two sisters, mother-in-law, husband, and son. In the first month of her campaign, she went back and forth across her large district and visited several towns more than once.

She met opposition to her campaign with a sense of humor. A Mexican-American woman came up to her and asked, "Are you Zaffirini?" Zaffirini answered, "Yes . . . What can I do to help you?" The woman said, "I saw bumper stickers on cars and trucks and I thought Zaffirini was a new Pizza Hut."

At one rally a man addressed her in Spanish, "You? Everybody knows that women are supposed to stay at home and clean house." Zaffirini laughed and said, "Yes, sir, that's exactly what I'm going to do. I did the dusting off in May, swept up in June, and I'm going to mop up in November."

Many journalists questioned her ability to win a big political race in South Texas. As election day approached, however, editorials across her twenty-county district began endorsing her campaign. She won by a landslide over a group of four Democrats and two Republicans. She was the first border resident elected to represent District 21 in twenty years. It was the first of three landslide victories for the Laredo resident.

## Senator with Many Names

During her first term in office, Zaffirini became the champion of the "momma agenda" in the Texas Legislature. Although told by her political advisers not to focus too much on the mother issue, Zaffirini said, "Some people look at legislation from the direction of 'Bubba.' I look at it from the direction of 'momma.'" People in Laredo refer to Zaffirini as *Señora Doña,* the Boss Lady. Her colleagues tease her about her "schoolteacher manners." She is called the "*madrina* (godmother) of Texas children" because of her emphasis on bills that affect the well-being of all children.

Zaffirini is just as committed to her own family as she is to passing laws in the Texas Legislature. She often commutes to Laredo from Austin so she can stay involved in her son's and husband's activities. One of her prized honors is a plaque for being "the best cooker in the whole world," presented by her son's kindergarten class. She not only cooks for her son and husband, but often bakes cookies or cakes for fellow legislators to thank them for giving her support on bills she introduced.


## Commitment to Constituents

Zaffirini has a simple system of preparing for each bill that comes before the legislature. She keeps a file on each bill that includes the bill itself, its pros and cons, and comments from her constituents. When she votes, she knows what is being voted on and the effect it will have on the state as well as in her district in South Texas. Zaffirini's well-trained staff organizes material in folders in order of priority. She knows each day what she needs

171

to accomplish and does not go to bed until those things are completed. On the average she sleeps only five hours a night.

In 1993 Lieutenant Governor Bob Bullock appointed Zaffirini to the Finance Committee, the Education Committee, and named her chairman of the Health and Human Services Committee. She was the first female Senate chair in thirty years and the first female chair of a major committee in the history of the Senate. The committee dealt with child protective services, immunization of children, services for people with mental illness and retardation, and similar programs.

In January 1997 Zaffirini was elected president pro tempore of the Texas Senate by her fellow legislators. She became the highest-ranking individual in state government after the governor and lieutenant governor. On April 19, 1997, she was the first Hispanic woman to serve as Governor for a Day. In June she was honored for having cast 18,457 consecutive votes. She had 100 percent attendance and voting records, the only person in Texas legislative history to do so. During six regular and twelve special sessions, she sponsored and passed 289 bills and forty-three resolutions, and co-sponsored and passed another 123 bills. Her legislative successes include passing bills to immunize 100 percent of Texas children; fund a statewide system of emergency medical services and trauma centers; suspend the driver's licenses of drunk drivers; keep radioactive waste dump sites out of State District 21; stop the increase of colonias; restrict minors' access to tobacco; and reform Medicaid, welfare, nursing homes, adoption, and child support.

## Awards and Honors

Senator Zaffirini has received more than 300 awards and honors for her legislative, public service, and professional work. *Texas Monthly* named her one of the "10 Best Legislators" in 1997. She was named Texas Heroine, Outstanding Legislator, and Friend of Business by the Texas Chamber of Commerce. The Texas Classroom Teachers Association named her Friend of Education. The Marine Corps League honored her for leadership, loyalty, and patriotism. Many organizations have named her Legislator of the Year. Her awards include the Children's Trust Fund of Texas Award for promoting and enhancing child/family-related issues; the Texas Catholic Conference Award of Excellence for outstanding ethics in public service; and the internationally prestigious Jose Maria Morelos y Pavon Medal of Merit for leadership in strengthening relations and promoting trade with Mexico.

Zaffirini feels that her greatest achievement has been "to pass bills that save lives and averted tragedies and provide a better future for the children and families of Texas. I focus on children and senior citizens and those who can't fight for themselves like children with mental retardation or mental illness." She championed an education bill that equalizes funds for all Texas schools so all children will have a chance for an excellent education regardless of where they live.

Because of her reputation and record as a senator, she is often asked if she would be interested in running for governor of Texas. "I'm not a career politician," she said. "I ran because there were needs to be addressed.

I'm an academician at heart. I love teaching, research and writing."

Zaffirini attributes her discipline and drive to her education at Ursuline Academy, her peers, her parents, and her husband. "Peer pressure does not have to be a negative thing," she says. "Children can help each other with positive help by encouraging and being a role model." She encourages students to "Always dream high, reach for the stars! If I can be senator, you can be governor."

"If Judy Pappas can do it, *anybody* can!" And Judith Pappas Zaffirini has done it all.

# Chapter Notes

## Christia V. Daniels Adair

**p. 1** "My parents . . ." Rogers, Mary Beth, et. al. *We Can Fly: Stories of Katherine Stinson and Other Gutsy Texas Women*. (Austin, Texas: Ellen C. Temple, 1983), p. 113.

**p. 2** "We dressed . . ." Winegarten, Ruthe. *Black Texas Women: A Sourcebook: Documents, Biographies, Timeline*. Janet G. Humphrey and Frieda Werden, consulting editors. (Austin, Texas: University of Texas Press, 1966), p. 85.
"You can learn . . ." *Ibid.*, p. 136.

**p. 4** "It just put . . ." *Ibid.*, p. 85.

**p. 5** "Some men say . . ." Taylor, A. Elizabeth. *Citizens at Last: The Woman Suffrage Movement in Texas*. (Austin, Texas: Ellen C. Temple, 1987), p. 181.
"I was offended . . ." Tyler, Ron, editor in chief, et al. *The New Handbook of Texas*. 6 vols. (Austin: The Texas State Historical Association, 1996), Vol. 1, p. 21.

**p. 6** "I never had a gun . . ." Rogers, p. 22.

**p. 7** "I bought . . ." Winegarten, Ruthe. *Governor Ann Richards and other Texas Women from Indians to Astronauts*. (Austin, Texas: Eakin Press, 1993), p. 117.

## Annie Webb Blanton

**p. 11** ". . . while I had . . ." Crawford, Ann Fears, and Crystal Sasse Ragsdale. *Women in Texas: Their Lives; Their Experiences; Their Accomplishments*. (Burnet, Texas: Eakin Press, 1982), p. 194.

**p. 13** "As I taught . . ." Cottrell, Debbie Mauldin. *Pioneer Educator: The Progressive Spirit of Annie Webb Blanton*. (College Station: Texas A&M University Press, 1993), p. 15.

**p. 14** "neither a college . . ." *Ibid.,* p. 21.

**p. 15** ". . . had carried his candidacy . . ." Crawford, p. 192.

**p. 17** "She is a woman . . ." *Ibid.,* p. 200.


### Mary Eleanor Brackenridge

**p. 20** "Women's clubs . . ." Winegarten, Ruthe. *Governor Ann Richards and other Texas Women from Indians to Astronauts.* (Austin, Texas: Eakin Press, 1993), p. 102.

**p. 21** Until her death . . . Menger, Johnowene Brackenridge Crutcher. *M. Eleanor Brackenridge, 1837-1924, A Third Generation Advocate of Education.* (M.A. thesis, Trinity University, 1964), pp. 27-28.
"I want to make . . ." *Ibid.,* p. 22.

**p. 23** "Unity is our strength." *Ibid.,* p. 45.
"instinct will make" Winegarten, p. 102.

**p. 24** ". . . born in the state." *Ibid.*

**p. 25** ". . . one of the most beautiful . . ." Menger, p. 63.

**p. 26** "Learn to do . . ." *Ibid.,* p. 129.


### Linda Chavez-Thompson

**p. 27** . . . person of color. Interview with Linda Chavez-Thompson, December 23, 1997. A person of color refers to all groups other than Anglo-Americans. At the writing of this book, it is the current politically correct term in reference to a diversified group: Asian Americans, Afro-Americans, Native Americans, etc.

**p. 29** "I'm a woman . . ." Bernstein, Harry. "Linda Chavez-Thompson: Is Revitalizing America's Labor Movement a Sicyphean Task?" *Los Angeles Times*, Sunday, February 4, 1996.

**p. 30** "It won't work . . ." Interview with Linda Chavez-Thompson.

**p. 31** "My mama says . . ." *Ibid.*

**p. 32** "I'll think about it . . ." *Ibid.*

**p. 34** ". . . ten pound knot . . ." *Ibid.*

**p. 35** "It was almost . . ." Franklin, Stephen. "Labor's Message Heard in Clear New Voice." *Chicago Tribune*, October 30, 1995.

**p. 36** "Anyone will tell . . ." Silverstein, Stuart. "Working Within Two Cultures." *Los Angeles Times*, October 27, 1995.
"each woman is born . . ." Interview.

### Sue Margaret Cousins

**p. 39** "I was trained . . ." Flynn, Robert, and Susan Russell. *When I was Just Your Age*. (Denton: University of North Texas Press, 1992), p. 166.

"You walked . . ." *Ibid.*, p. 161.

"It just left me . . ." *Ibid.*, p. 160.

**p. 40** . . . a career in writing and editing for women's . . . Mundt, Shirley M. "Margaret Cousins." *American Magazine Journalists 1900-1960*, Sam G. Riley, ed. *Dictionary of Literary Biography*, Vol. 137, Second Series. (Detroit: Gail Researchers, Inc., 1994), p. 54.

"Margaret stole them . . ." Flynn, p. 165.

**p. 41** . . . American history and journalism . . . Mundt, p. 54.

**p. 45** "Of all the writers . . ." Cousins, Margaret. *Christmas Keepers: Eight Memorable Stories from the 40's and 50's*. (San Antonio: Corona Publishing Company, 1996), p. vii.

"I think if you don't . . ." Flynn, p. 167.

"I think for Maggie . . ." Rigler, Judyth. "Tribute: a Legend." SA Life, *San Antonio Express News*, August 3, 1996, p. 2F.

"Editorially, there was nothing . . ." Mundt, p. 59.

### Olive Ann Oatman Fairchild

**p. 48** ". . . drew him back . . ." McLeRoy, Sherrie S. *Red River Women*. (Plano, Texas: Republic of Texas Press, 1996), p. 104.

"The facts connected . . ." Pettid, Edward J., ed. "Olives Ann Oatman's Lecture Notes and the Oatman Bibliography." *San Bernardino County Museum Association Quarterly*, Vol. XVI, No. 2, Winter 1968. p 1.

"The Lord had . . ." "The Oatman Story." *Arizona Highways*, XLIV, November 1968, p. 5.

**p. 51** "Well, there is one thing . . ." Stratton, R.B. *Captivity of the Oatman Girls*. (Lincoln: University of Nebraska, 1983), p. 74.

"Mother, mother . . ." *Ibid.*, p. 79.

**p. 52** "Suddenly as a clap . . ." *Ibid.*, p. 86.

"Mother, O mother . . ." *Ibid.*, p. 87.

**p. 53** "That night . . ." Pettid, p. 14.

"It was our lot . . ." Stratton, p. 138.

**p. 54** . . . in a rat's hole. Koeber, A. L. *Handbook of Indians of California*. (Berkeley: California Book Company, 1946), p. 729.

### Frances Tarlton "Sissy" Farenthold

**p. 57** . . . that she could not read. Telephone interview with Frances Tarlton Farenthold, October 17, 1997.

**p. 59** "A woman must . . ." Farenthold, Frances Tarlton. Papers, 1944-

1992. Center for American History, University of Texas at Austin. Scrap-book 1984.

**p. 60** "If you read . . ." Telephone interview.
"I just couldn't . . ." Farenthold, Scrapbook 1982.

**p. 61** "It was the most . . ." Farenthold, Frances Tarlton "Sissy."
Biographical file, Center for American History, University of Texas at Austin.
"Lower your skirts . . ." *Ibid.*

**p. 62** "When you have handed . . ." Frances T. Farenthold, letter to
Shirley Hendrix, February 8, 1979, Farenthold Papers.
"advocate of lost causes" Crawford, Ann Fears, and Crystal Sasse
Ragsdale. *Women in Texas: Their Lives; Their Experiences; Their
Accomplishments.* (Burnet, Texas: Eakin Press, 1982), p. 289.

**p. 63** "den mother of . . ." Farenthold Papers.

**p. 64** ". . . I went to a girl's . . ." Crawford, p. 292.

**p. 65** ". . . there wasn't a role model . . ." Lasher, Patricia. *Texas
Women: Interviews and Images.* Photographs by Beverly Bentley. (Austin,
Texas: Shoal Creek Publishers, Inc., 1980), p. 43.
"The answer should be . . ." *Ibid.*

**p. 66** "Ignorance reinforces . . ." Brockway, Rughanne. " 'Sissy'
Farenthold Urges Women to Be Tenacious." *Lubbock Avalanche Journal*, Sun-day, October 20, 1980. Farenthold Papers, Scrapbook 1980.
". . . to continue to open doors . . ." Cortez, Laura, and David
Real. "Farenthold: Time for Change." *San Antonio Light*, August 10, 1980.

### Bette Nesmith Graham
**p. 69** ". . . women must . . ." Lasher, Patricia. *Texas Women: Interviews
and Images.* Photographs by Beverly Bentley. (Austin, Texas: Shoal Creek
Publishers, Inc., 1980), p. 51.

**p. 70** "I decided . . ." Rogers, Mary Beth, et al. *We Can Fly: Stories of
Katherine Stinson and Other Gutsy Texas Women.* (Austin, Texas: Ellen C.
Temple, 1983), p. 90.

**p. 71** "It was hard . . ." Lasher, p. 50.

**p. 72** ". . . to overcome the fear . . ." Rogers, p. 90.

**p. 74** ". . . of personal and corporate growth on which . . ." Lasher, p.
51.
"Most people . . ." Rogers, p. 97.

### Oveta Culp Hobby
**p. 77** "My father expected . . ." Lasher, Patricia. *Texas Women: Inter-*

*views and Images*. Photographs by Beverly Bentley. (Austin, Texas: Shoal Creek Publishers, Inc., 1980), p. 74.

"My father taught me . . ." Hurt, Harry III. "The Last of the Great Ladies." *Texas Monthly*, October 1978, p. 146.

"Girls, you will . . ." Hobby, Oveta Culp. Center for American History, University of Texas at Austin.

**p. 78** "I'll bet I've read . . ." Hobby, Oveta Culp. Scrapbook.

**p. 79** Her collection included ... Hobby, William Pettus, Jr. "Oveta Culp Hobby." *The New Handbook of Texas*. 6 vols. (Austin: The Texas State Historical Association), Vol. 3, p. 637b.

". . . my sister's clothing . . ." Lasher, p. 74.

**p. 80** "Will, she'll embarrass . . ." Hobby, p. 638a.

**p. 81** "You must do . . ." *Ibid.*

**p. 82** "It would never have . . ." *Ibid.*

". . . had a tremendous . . ." Lasher, p. 76.

**p. 83** ". . . the best man . . ." Scrapbook.

**p. 84** "The woman who . . ." *Ibid.*

"Oh, it's the easiest . . ." *Ibid.*

### Mary Austin Holley

**p. 87** "This theme of . . ." Lee, Rebecca Smith. *Mary Austin Holley, a biography*. (Austin: University of Texas Press, 1962), p. 223.

**p. 90** "a child of misfortune . . ." Holley, Mary Austin. *Texas* (reprint). (Austin, Texas: The Texas State Historical Association, 1985), n.p.

**p. 92** "I little anticipated . . ." Hatcher, Mattie Austin. *Letters of an Early American Traveller: Mary Austin Holley, Her Life and Works 1784-1846*. (Dallas, Texas: Southwest Press, 1933), p. 56.

### Elizabeth E. "Lizzie" Johnson

**p. 95** ". . .the trip [Chisholm Trail] . . ." Shelton, Emily Jones. "Lizzie E. Johnson: A Cattle Queen of Texas." *The Southwestern Historical Quarterly*, Vol. L, July 1946 to April 1947, p. 357.

"austere and firm" *Ibid.*, p. 350.

**p. 98** "would keep his too long . . ." Johnson, Elizabeth E. Biographical File. Center for American History, University of Texas at Austin.

"while Hezekiah . . ." Shelton, p. 356.

**p. 100** She brought Williams back ... Biographical file.

"When he got real sick . . ." *Ibid.*

**p. 101** "I loved . . ." *Ibid.*

"Hello, you old . . ." Shelton, p. 362.
"She sure didn't like . . ." Biographical file.

### Margaret Virginia "Margo" Jones

**p. 105** "I was lucky . . ." Jones, Margo. *Theatre-in-the-Round*. (Westport, Connecticut: Greenwood Press, 1970), p. 3.

**p. 106** "I didn't think . . ." Sheehy, Helen. *Margo: The Life and Theatre of Margo Jones*. (Dallas: Southern Methodist University Press, 1989), p. 8.

**p. 108** "My first glimpse . . ." *Ibid.*, p. 22.
"I saw no reason . . ." *Ibid.*, p. 28.

**p. 109** "No, honey, . . ." *Ibid.*, p. 42.
"Put up or . . ." Rogers, Mary Beth, et al. *We Can Fly: Stories of Katherine Stinson and Other Gutsy Texas Women*. (Austin, Texas: Ellen C. Temple, 1983), p. 55.
"I ... like to think . . ." Sheehy, p. 108.

### Lucy Ann Thornton Kidd-Key

**p. 113** "I have an abiding . . ." McLeRoy, Sherrie S. *Red River Women*. Women of the West Series. (Plano, Texas: Republic of Texas Press, 1996), p. 129.
Lucy helped make money . . . *Ibid.*, p. 132.

**p. 115** ". . . the special mission of art education." Berry, Maggie. Letter to *Dallas Morning News* (Dallas, Texas), reprinted in the *Sherman Daily Democrat* (Sherman, Texas), January 24, 1916.

**p. 116** "a Christian lady . . ." *Sherman Daily Democrat*, April 11, 1888.

**p. 118** "This is the only . . ." *Catalogue of North Texas Female College and Conservatory of Music,* Sherman, Texas, 1905-06, p.2.

**p. 119** "If a woman has brains . . ." McLeRoy, p. 142
". . . Still guards them from all harm." *"The Forget-Me-Not"* Yearbook, 1908-1909, p. 78.

**p. 121** "To live in the world . . ." Norfleet, Helen. Class of 1910. "Mrs. Lucy A. Kidd-Key and the Beauty of Personality," *The Key*, November 1917, p. 7.

### Jane Yelvington McCallum

**p. 123** "bad men were . . ." Humphrey, Janet G. *A Texas Suffragist: Diaries and Writings of Jane Y. McCallum*. (Austin, Texas: Ellen C. Temple, 1988), p. 17.
**p. 124** "If a woman . . ." Rogers, Mary Beth, et al. *We Can Fly: Stories of Katherine Stinson and Other Gutsy Texas Women*. (Austin, Texas: Ellen C. Temple, 1983), p. 109.

". . . hold the enviable . . ." Humphrey, p. 19.
"establish a little . . ." *Ibid.*, p. 21.

**p. 126** "politically classified . . ." *Ibid.*, p. 30.

**p. 128** "Then you should be . . ." Rogers, p. 101.
"You apologize . . ." *Ibid.*, p. 103.

**p. 129** ". . . surely a convincing . . ." Crawford, Ann Fears, and Crystal Sasse Ragsdale. *Women in Texas: Their Lives; Their Experiences; Their Accomplishments.* (Burnet, Texas: Eakin Press, 1982), p. 227.

**p. 130** "never vote for a woman . . ." *Ibid.*, p. 230.
"We asked for . . ." Humphrey, n.p.


*Patricia McCormick*
**p. 133** "I'm ambitious . . ." McCormick, Patricia. *Patricia McCormick, Lady Bullfighter: The Autobiography of the North American Matador.* (New York: Henry Holt and Company, 1954), p. 45.
"barbaric use" *Ibid.*, p. 27.
"Dreams are fine . . ." *Ibid.*, p. 37

**p. 134** "You have to get over . . ." *Ibid.*, p. 44.

**p. 136** "to becoming a true . . ." Lea, Tom. *Bullfight Manual for Spectators.* (El Paso, Texas: Carl Hertzog, 1957), p. 3.

**p. 137** "the bravery of the bull . . ." *Ibid.*

**p. 139** "honey blonde hair" McCormick, Patricia. Biographical file. Center for American History, University of Texas at Austin.
"When she is working . . ." McCormick, p. 95.

**p. 140** "women should not . . ." Murray, Jack. "Texas Girl Explains 'Call' to Bull Ring." *Los Angeles Times*, n.d.
"the one I am inside . . ." McCormick, p. 4.

**p. 141** "Had she not . . ." McCormick, Particia. "A Brave Matadora Explains the Bullfight." *Sports Illustrated*, March 11, 1963, p. 39.
"Bullfighting has no . . ." Warren, Mary Stuart. "Papa Is an Oilman . . . But Nothing so Tame for Pat." *Daily Oil News*, 1954, n.p.
"Follow your goals . . ." Murphy, Hank. "Lady bullfighter carves niche in male domain." *Big Spring Herald*, n.d.


*Irma Rangel*
**p. 144** "We grew up . . ." Crawford, Ann Fears, and Crystal Sasse Ragsdale. *Women in Texas: Their Lives; Their Experiences; Their Accomplishments.* (Burnet, Texas: Eakin Press, 1982), p. 332.

**p. 146** . . . with their daughters. Interview with State Representative Irma Rangel, November 4, 1997.

**p. 147** "their ignorance . . ." *Ibid.*

**p. 148** "See, you didn't . . ." *Ibid.*

**p. 149** "I am not going . . ." *Ibid.*
"Nothing is easy . . ." *Ibid.*
"But still, the first . . ." *Ibid.*

**p. 151** "[she] suddenly realized . . ." *Ibid.*
"whatever [she] said . . ." *Ibid.*
"Hey, someone . . ." *The Capitol of Texas: A Legend Is Reborn* by staff members of the *Reborn* by staff members of the (Atlanta, Georgia: Longstreet Press, Inc., 1995), p. 132.

**p. 152** "I think I've gained . . ." Interview.
"I was only . . ." *Ibid.*
"to convince students . . ." *Ibid.*

### Elizabeth Marion Watson
**p. 155** "Do not become . . ." Strandberg, Keith W. "Police Chief Elizabeth M. Watson." *Law Enforcement Technology*, February 1993, p. 24.
"Do you know . . ." Watson, Elizabeth M. Biographical file. Austin History Center, Austin, Texas.

**p. 156** "that [they] could . . ." Shapiro, Walter. "Performing Our Image As a Chief." *Time*, November, 26, 1990, p.82.
". . . 'make-up' referred to cosmetics." Interview with Elizabeth M. Watson, December 3, 1997.

**p. 157** "real job." *Ibid.*

**p. 158** "Playing a dumb . . ." Biographical file.

**p. 159** "just like the old West" Shapiro, p. 82.
"too tough a job . . ." Interview.
"My sense was . . ." *Ibid.*

**p. 161** "It is an awesome . . ." Shapiro, p. 80.
"The community is going . . ." Biographical file.

**p. 162** "partly because it was . . ." *Ibid.*
"I don't care where . . ." Interview.
Watson sees it as an ... *Ibid.*

**p. 163** "to get into the field . . ." Strandberg, p. 25.

*Judith Zaffirini*

**p. 165** "Judy Pappas . . ." Interview with Senator Judith Zaffirini, December 12, 1997.

**p. 166** "I have experienced . . ." Scaperlanda, Maria Ruiz. "South Texas Interview with Senator Judith Zaffirini, December 12, 1997.

**p. 167** "If you do not . . ." Interview.
"And the moral of . . ." *Ibid.*

**p. 168** "There have been many . . ." Scaperlanda, p. 16.

**p. 169** ". . . I thought it was . . ." Gordon, Dona. "15,000 and Still Counting: The Tireless Texan." *State Legislatures*, July/August 1997. p. 17.
"little blessing is . . ." Scaperlanda 16.
"to prioritize my work . . ." Zaffirini, Judith. Biographical file. Center for American History, University of Texas at Austin.

**p. 170** "I saw bumper stickers . . ." Interview.
"Yes sir, that's . . ." Biographical file.

**p. 171** "Some people look . . ." Davidson, Bruce. "Zaffirini Championing State 'Momma Agenda.'" *San Antonio Express-News*. June 25, 1989, n.p.

**p. 173** . . . promoting trade with Mexico. Senator Judith Zaffirini Profile, November 20, 1997. Courtesy of Senator Judith Zaffirini.
"to pass bills . . ." Interview.
"I'm not a career . . ." Deihl, Kemper. "Zaffirini Content as a Senator . . ." *San Antonio Express-News,* August 22, 1993, n.p.

**p. 174** "Children can . . ." Interview.
"Always dream high . . ." "Zaffirini urges students to 'reach for the stars.'" *Sentinel*, Crystal City, Texas, Thursday, October, 16, 1997, n.p.
"If Judy Pappas . . ." Interview.

# Bibliography

Bennett, Michele and Barbara. *Twenty-Two Texas Women: Strong, Tough, and Independent*. Austin, Texas: Eakin Press, 1996.

Cottrell, Debbie Mauldin. *Pioneer Educator: The Progressive Spirit of Annie Webb Blanton*. College Station: Texas A&M University Press, 1993.

Crawford, Ann Fears, and Crystal Sasse Ragsdale. *Women in Texas: Their Lives; Their Experiences; Their Accomplishments*. Burnet, Texas: Eakin Press, 1982.

Downs, Fane, and Nancy Baker Jones, eds. *Women and Texas History, Selected Essays*. Austin: Texas State Historical Association, 1993.

Flynn, Robert, and Susan Russell. *When I was Just Your Age*. Denton: University of North Texas Press, 1992.

Gurasich, Marj. *Did you ever . . . meet a Texas hero?* Austin, Texas: Eakin Press, 1992.

Holley, Mary Austin. *Texas*. Reprint. Austin, Texas: The Texas State Historical Association, 1985.

Humphrey, Janet G. *A Texas Suffragist: Diaries and Writings of Jane Y. McCallum*. Austin, Texas: Ellen C. Temple, 1988.

Lasher, Patricia. *Texas Women: Interviews and Images*. Photographs by Beverley Bentley. Austin, Texas: Shoal Creek Publishers, Inc.,1980.

Lee, Rebecca Smith. *Mary Austin Holley, A Biography*. Austin, Texas: University of Texas Press, 1962.

McLeRoy, Sherrie S. *Red River Women*. Plano, Texas: Republic of Texas Press, 1996.

Rogers, Mary Beth, et al. *We Can Fly: Stories of Katherine Stinson and Other Gutsy Texas Women*. Austin, Texas: Ellen C. Temple, 1983.

Seligman, Claudia Dee. *Texas Women: Legends in Their Own Time*. Dallas: Hendrick-Long Publishing Company, 1994.

Sheehy, Helen. *Margo: The Life and Theatre of Margo Jones*. Dallas: Southern Methodist University Press, 1989.

Taylor, A. Elizabeth. *Citizens at Last: The Woman Suffrage Movement in Texas*. Austin, Texas: Ellen C. Temple, 1987.

Winegarten, Ruthe. *Black Texas Women: A Sourcebook: Documents, Biographies, Timeline*. Janet G. Humphrey and Frieda Werden, consulting editors. Austin: University of Texas Press, 1996.

———. *Finder's Guide to the Texas Women: A Celebration of History Exhibit Archives*. Denton, Texas: Texas Woman's University Library, 1984.

———. *Governor Ann Richards and other Texas Women from Indians to Astronauts*. Austin, Texas: Eakin Press, 1993.

# Suggested Activities

The following activities are for both male and female students to bring awareness to the obstacles women have had or will have to overcome to enter the work force.

1. Have a contest in which students find as many women firsts as they can locate using both school and public libraries.

2. Students research a specific profession or job and explain why women are or are not hired in that area.

3. Students develop a survey, collect data, and report the different types of employment of parents in the classroom; categorize the careers by those that males dominate and those females dominate; explain why some do not fit into one category.

4. Students work as a class in cooperative groups or independently to write a questionnaire for an oral history of an older woman in their families; each student conducts an interview, writes the history, and illustrates it with family photographs.

5. Students write an accurate "help wanted" ad for a job they would like to have; include requirements such as education, type of work, license, approximate salary, etc.

WBN

WBU